CHOPPED
HARLEYS

CHOPPED HARLEYS

50 Years of Rebellious Motorcycles

JOHN CARROLL

Photographs by GARRY STUART

PUBLISHED BY

SALAMANDER BOOKS LIMITED

LONDON

A Salamander Book

Published by Salamander Books Ltd.
129–137 York Way
London N7 9LG
United Kingdom

1 3 5 7 9 8 6 4 2

Distributed by Random House Value Publishing, Inc.
201 East 50th Street
New York, NY 10022.
http://www.randomhouse.com/

A CIP catalog record for this book is available from the Library of Congress.

ISBN 0-517-18775-2

Acknowledgments
Both author and photographer are indebted to all those who allowed their bikes to be
photographed for this book, and to whoever invented the hacksaw. Phil Piper's
assistance with archive material (and the author's 45 chop!) is greatly appreciated.

Credits
Editor: Dennis Cove
Designer: John Heritage
Photographer: Garry Stuart
Filmset by SX Composing DTP, England
Color reproduction by Dah Hua Printing Press, Hong Kong
Printed in France

Additional captions
1 Chopper Club patch
2 Steve Green's 96 cubic inch S & S chopper
4 Shovelhead chop at Daytona
6 Daytona street scene
8 The classic chopper silhouette
10 Psychedelic Panhead chop

CONTENTS

FOREWORD

I WOULD LIKE TO think that this book – because it's about choppers and nothing else – is different from a lot of books about Harleys. This is no model-by-model history of the Milwaukee marque. It documents a slice of Harley–Davidson action that the factory would rather didn't exist, although if there had been no 'One-Percenters' and no notoriety it is likely that the fad for Harley ownership of recent years would not have occurred. Nowadays the factory builds bikes and sells clothing clearly inspired by the biker sub-culture. Mr and Mrs Cleancut are buying into Harley's watered-down interpretation of the outlaw biker lifestyle when they step across the dealer's threshold.

Chopping a Harley involves a much greater degree of commitment to the bike in question and there's much more at stake than the resale value. The guys who seriously want to ride a chopper will overcome all obstacles in order to do so. It's a long way from a couple of crates of swapmeet parts or a worn out stocker to splitting lanes on a finished chopper. I hope in reading this book you'll be heartened by the fact that I know exactly how far it is, as the chopper pictured on this page is my bike. It's a built-from-scratch, rigid flathead that grew out of an olive drab WLC (Canadian Army 45) engine and transmission. New wheel rims were laced to swapmeet hubs, yokes were made from billet alloy for the secondhand telescopic forks. A custom rear fender was shortened to suit the lines of the frame that had been made to measure and to accept the diverse selection of components including an Evo Sportster gas

Left: *Upswept fishtail exhaust pipes on the Captain America Panhead replica chop.*
Above: *The author's rigid chop is based around a 45 cubic inch WLC and traditionally styled – with concessions to the 1990s.*

tank. The handlebars, brake master cylinder, grips, headlight, tail light and numerous small parts came over the counter at custom shops and so it went on. The forward controls were made to measure. The seat is a one-off but, after a lot of help from good friends, the machine was ready for paint. Then there were the hassles of getting a license plate but in the end every cent, every drop of sweat and all the worry was worthwhile.

Anyway, the flathead ain't got the biggest engine, it hasn't had the most money spent on it, and it definitely isn't the fanciest in this book. It is my bike: rigid frame, Sportster tank way up high, apehanger bars, solo seat, jockey shift, suicide clutch, and flame paint. Its lines are intended to be timeless, albeit with a few modern touches, and while the same style of bike might have looked cool with a Panhead motor, here in Europe there's a lot of respect for the 45 cubic inch flathead. They ain't called 'Liberators' for nothing. Harleys are often described as the 'Freedom Machine' and in the case of the 45 flathead it

really is the truth. One generation of Americans and Canadians rode them in World War II to help keep Europe free and I think it's entirely appropriate that the engines should provide the power for the freedom machines of another generation.

I believe that my motivation to have my own chopper is not dissimilar to that of many others. For me it was the culmination of a dream, one nurtured since the first time I stumbled across *Street Chopper* magazine and opened Hunter Thompson's book years ago while still at school. Later the mathematics teacher confiscated Thompson's book when he found me reading it in his lesson. At the same place the Latin teacher told me I was going nowhere; he taught a dead language and I knew I'd be riding a chopper – who was going nowhere? That's what did it for me. How about you?

The other reason this book is different is that it chronicles the development of something altogether imprecise. Choppers were often rebuilt and rebuilt again and each decade belongs to a different generation of riders. Magazines and custom parts catalogs are the only genuine archive material, the only exception being a handful of movies.

This book has a primarily American perspective simply because that is where choppers originated but it is worth pointing out that in Europe the chopper-thing really got started in the early Seventies and initially copied American styles using many imported parts. Gradually though styles unique to Europe developed. The Swedes are noted for building extremely long forked choppers, the British still happily build classy choppers with almost any type of motorcycle engine, and there's currently a strong style for 'Streetfighters' – Harleys with performance sports bike front ends and mono-shocks. Choppers: ever evolving indeed.

INTRODUCTION

ASK MOST PEOPLE what a chopper is and likely as not they'll come up with something about 'a motorcycle with long forks'. Press them further and they'll concede it's usually ridden by a 'long haired biker-type'. There's few people behind a windshield who at one time or another haven't had their senses assaulted by the sight of a chopper riding club, loud and proud, jamming it on, passing the traffic. Straight citizens gaze, mouths agape, at once both fascinated and reviled... 'I mean, what's it actually like to ride one of those things?'

There's a pleasant irony in all this because if you ask a motorcyclist, rather than a biker – bikers are a rare breed, Harley riders are a dime a dozen – what a chopper is, he may well describe them as being noisy, dangerous, thrown together and an affront to respectable motorcycling or conjure up other negative images. Sure he'll tell you what a sports bike, a trail bike, an enduro bike, a roadster, a race replica, a tourer or a moped are but the truth is that to the non-motorcycling public these are all just 'motorcycles' while choppers are different. Choppers are choppers. Adding to the irony of the situation is that there were no big factories with teams of engineers working on the designs for choppers as there were (and are) for every other type of motorcycle without exception. There are no lovingly produced brochures listing the selling points and desirable features. There are no sheets or books of the specifications and minutiae of the machine's components. There's no advertising campaigns and yet despite all this the chopper is the most recognizable type of motorcycle in

Left: *Chris Brown of East Anglia, UK, riding his chopped Harley and photographed head-on in a style similar to that of the biker paintings of artist David Mann.*

the world... 'That ain't no motorcycle, baby, that's a chopper.'

The chopper's origins are distant and imprecise – the style evolved out of other motorcycles with the addition of a few acid-influenced dreams and marijuana-inspired thoughts. While it is hard to pinpoint its conception exactly, acceptance (by some) of the chopper as *bona fide* is found in unorthodox places. The Angels refer to standard 74s as 'garbage wagons' and Bylaw Number 11 of the charter is a put-down in the grand manner: 'An Angel cannot wear the colors while riding on a garbage wagon with a non-Angel'. This, which is quoted from Hunter S. Thompson in 1966, illustrates how the chopper as a distinct type of motorcycle, became more than simply acknowledged but mandatory within that club. In the vernacular of that time a garbage wagon was a stock Harley–Davidson still equipped with windshield and panniers, a 74 was a 74 cubic inch displacement Harley–Davidson. In other words only choppers were acceptable for club members to be seen on. These decidedly unofficial and almost underground origins as the transport of the Hells Angels and the numerous other clubs of that era including the Satan's Slaves, Gypsy Jokers, Satan's Sinners and the Jokers Out Of Hell amongst others would ensure that motorcycles and motorcycling would never be the same again. It would mean that choppers appeared on the front pages of newspapers across the western world. From there it was but a short step to the chopper making its appearance in movies; the biker on a chopper just like the cowboy on his horse became both hero and anti-hero dependent on the script writer's whim. The marked similarity between the old time outlaws such as Jesse James and Billy the Kid wasn't lost on the new generation of saddle tramps either and it isn't

implausible to suggest both groups have similar origins, come from similar socio-economic backgrounds and are divided only by the centuries of their respective eras. They were wild and rowdy times; much of everything was new, especially the vehicles, the innovations and maybe the dreams.

While some may see chopper riders as the last cowboys, others see them as the last pirates, swashbucklers traversing the globe on Harleys. It's surely no accident that the colors of many clubs feature derivations of the Jolly Roger, and that many male bikers had their left ear pierced pirate-fashion long before it was fashionable in the mainstream. Pirates, cowboys, gipsies, tramps or thieves, this enigma on wheels rolls on. It's a never-ending journey, as new as tomorrow and as old as time itself, tempered by action, danger and the elements, in search of freedom and romance. A longneck and a dollar for the juke box, 'ladies love outlaws' (and hot looking choppers)...ain't it the truth?

The choppers featured in this book have all been photographed in the last few years and selected for this book as being representative of the era of the chapter in which they appear. Some are genuine, unrestored examples of old-time choppers; others are replicas of days long gone; still more are bikes from that era which have been restored or which have gradually evolved as the decades, like the miles, slipped by. There are choppers photographed at the big annual biker gatherings: Daytona in the spring and Sturgis before the fall; and there are bikes from Colorado and California seen in their home states. There are choppers too from Europe, where the passion for choppers thrives ever since Peter Fonda and Dennis Hopper's movie and their characters, Wyatt and Billy, exported notions of long forks, free living and endless blacktop right around the globe.

1946–1959

WHERE IT ALL BEGAN

THE ORIGINS OF THE CHOPPER are inextricably linked with the period of American motorcycling that straddled World War II. As the country emerged from the depths of the Depression, motorcycling again became a popular pastime and the establishment of Class C gave it a wider appeal in that 'ordinary' riders could compete without the expense of specialist race bikes. Class C and the staging of a number of AMA-sanctioned 100- and 200-mile National races in places like Savannah, Georgia, and Daytona, Florida, started to attract huge crowds of spectators. Many riders emulated the style of the mildly modified race bikes for street use – Class C rules meant that race bikes were required to be

Left: *A Fifties bobber based around a Knucklehead motor and frame but with a later Hydra-Glide front end.*
Below: *A New York bobber based around a WLDR – a pre-war 45 cubic inch flathead Harley. Fenders are cut back to a minimum.*

street legal prior to the race – so that what can be termed pre-war customs were usually bikes modified with a cut-down or removed front fender and bobtailed – later shortened to bobbed – rear fender. Sometimes a front fender was fitted to the back so that flared end was much further around the wheel than normal and a pillion pad put on that, the whole being supported by a modified or specifically fabricated fender strut. These modifications were made to both Harley–Davidson and Indian motorcycles reflecting

Above: *Dan Hawkins' early-style Knuckle-head chop is basically a cut-down or 'chopped' stock FL Knucklehead with the exception of the 21 inch diameter front wheel, apehangers, tail light and the jockey shift arrangement and the lustrous purple paint.*

the fact that both were popular American bikes and that much of the racetrack rivalry was between the motorcycles of the two companies. Racing in particular and motorcycling in general were to be curtailed by the outbreak of World War II for the USA with the Japanese airstrike against Pearl Harbor in Hawaii.

Another important pre-war development was the 1936 launch of the overhead-valve EL model of 61 cubic inches displacement. This was a fast road bike and although its production span was also interrupted by the war it was to have a major effect on motorcycling. Its introduction was one of the factors that gave Harley–Davidson a significant advantage over its last domestic competitor, Indian of Springfield, Massachusets.

Following the defeat of Japan, US servicemen started coming home and many of them were looking for ways to spend their mustering out pay and let off steam after a few years in uniform. Harley–Davidson resumed production of the overhead-valve EL models albeit with a few modifications including redesigned tail lights and tank-mounted dashes. (Later both styles of lights and dashes would appear on custom bikes.) The war had left a distinct influence on motorcycling in other ways; it led to the superstition about green Harleys being unlucky. Despatch riders were often considered a target by the enemy because they were likely to be carrying important information as well as having to contend with dangerous journeys, land mines, and wires strung across the road to decapitate them in forward areas. The fact that one of the fascist enemies had been Japan meant that later the new-fangled

Japanese manufactured bikes would be derided as 'Jap Crap' and give rise to T-shirts and bumper stickers that bore slogans that read: 'Honda, Kawasaki, Suzuki, Yamaha – from the people who brought you Pearl Harbor'. Wino Willie Forkner, a former waist gunner and engineer in the 7th Air Force and later a charter member of Boozefighters MC – one of the earliest clubs – summed the attitude up in a 1986 interview in *Easyriders* magazine: "Yeah, well those damned riceheads. Son of a bitch, I don't understand how, if we won that damned war, it don't look like it. That's the bitch of it – they got the whole country here. It's amazing, I still can't believe it but I guess that's what politics is all about."

Of the survivors like Wino Willie, who came home and started riding motorcycles again, for some it was back to normal and back to AMA-sanctioned events. For others it wasn't so straightforward. Motorcycle club uniforms and rally games wouldn't have held the same appeal to restless combat veterans and those who'd buried their comrades in Europe and the Pacific Islands. The author of *From Here to Eternity*, James Jones, summed it up as follows:

'About the last thing to go was the sense of *esprit*. That was the hardest thing to let go of, because there was nothing in civilian life that could replace it. The love and understanding of men for men in dangerous times and places and situations. Just as there was nothing in civilian life that could replace the heavy, turgid day-to-day excitement of danger. Families and other civilian types would never understand that sense of *esprit* any more than they would understand the excitement of the danger.'

Some guys found what they were looking for in the saddle of a big motorcycle, with equally restless buddies and the endless blacktop – for better or worse the world had changed. Ed Maye, a Colorado resident, mustered out of the US Navy in 1946 and bought a 74 cubic inch Knucklehead. In 1996, while watching Harleys leaving Severance, Colorado, he recalled the back cylinder fouling the plug, grinding valve seats and re-ringing pistons and how, on a long run, occasionally the rider had to "shut the throttle off, then open it up to oil the top end". He recalled the vibrations transmitted to the rider from springer forks less fondly: "Hoff, a crazy nut, and I came back from Phoenix almost non-stop and my hands swelled right up."

The first post-war Daytona 200 was run in 1947 the same year as the AMA rally, races and Gypsy Tour in Hollister, California. This hitherto unremarkable event was about to become indelibly inked into the history books. Depending on which publications are consulted the goings-on at Hollister in 1947 over the Fourth of July weekend were anything from a full scale riot to little more than an amount of general rowdiness and beer drinking. *The San Francisco Chronicle* of Monday July 7, 1947 described it as 'The 40 hours that shook Hollister'. The lines

Right: *The combination of stock parts such as the fender-less springer forks, springs and ride-control assembly taken back to basics and chromed, combined with non-stock parts such as the high mounted headlamp and modified handlebars is nothing short of elegant.*

between fact and fiction have been blurred by time and the fact that *Life* magazine and subsequently also a movie-maker, Stanley Kramer, both picked up on the incident. Otherwise it probably would have faded into obscurity as the newsprint yellowed. The beer drinking, spinning donuts, racing in the street and a few arrests for drunkenness would have simply been put down to 'the boys having too much fun'. Instead the result was the 1953 Columbia Pictures film *The Wild One*. It starred Marlon Brando and Lee Marvin and, regardless of its interpretation of the facts, the film was pivotal in a number of respects – it set the style for future motor-cyclists in terms of clothing and bikes. Brando as the now legendary Johnny wore a

peaked cap and Highway Patrol jacket while Marvin as his rival was every inch the up and coming outlaw biker in his sleeveless jacket, scruffy beard, cap comforter and goggles. Brando's Johnny fronted the Black Rebels MC and rode a Triumph twin while Marvin did the same for the Beetles MC from the sad-dle of a chopped hog. As an aside, the latter club name is where the British pop group The Beatles took their name from.

Apart from inspiring hundreds of young-sters to copy the rider's styles of both clothes and motorcycles, the film, on a wider scale, incurred the wrath of an America edging its way towards McCarthyism. The country was become concerned about destabilization and to some people the film appeared to be

Right: *Jockey shift gear levers are so called because the rider reaches back behind his leg to shift, like a horse-racing jockey with whip.*
Below: *The race-style pillion pad is mounted on the shortened or 'bobbed' rear fender along with a classic Sparto tail light.*

Right: *James Brusca's classic Knucklehead chop is based around the frame, forks and engine of a 1947 FL Big Twin Harley although the leopard skin paint scheme, applied by Rick's Super Paint of Freehold, New Jersey, is considerably more modern.*

The chopper in question was presumably a post-war Knucklehead, 74 cubic inch variants of which were made in 1941 and 1946–47 or a 1948 Panhead as these were the only years of 74 cubic inch Harleys made with springer forks. Had it already been fitted with telescopic forks there would have been little point in changing the front ends.

Above: *To keep the lines of the chop clean, the handlebars follow the line of the forks exactly.* **Left:** *Barbie rides this chopper because, as the owner put it: "She was the first [doll] to make her way into American hearts." Road Pirates is a club dedicated to old choppers.*

Close examination of the photographs from Hollister at the time in *The San Francisco Chronicle* show pre-war big twin Harleys with the front fenders removed, wide dresser bars on Flanders risers, and at least one with a neatly bobbed rear fender cut back as far as the saddlebag hangers and fitted with a front fender trim. Class rides. The telescopic forked Harley later seen in the film *The Wild One* is treated similarly although these machines were not in production in 1947.

British bikes were seen as competition to the two remaining American domestic manufacturers but were also a source of parts to use on a chopper. H.R. Kaye describes an early 74 cubic inch chopper in his book *A Place in Hell* about the early days (although the period described is imprecisely dated):

'It was a masterpiece! The front fender had been removed and a Triumph front end installed. The rear fender was bobbed and chromed. It had dual headlights, apehangers, a custom tank and small leather saddle that had been pirated from an English racing machine. It had been painted black and polished to a blinding sheen. The engine was clean and neat as a pin.'

an abomination that seemingly promoted subversion and anti-social behaviour. It implied that all motorcyclists were no-good hoodlums who were intent only on disrupting American life. This suggestion had already been made after the actual Hollister incident and the American Motorcyclist Association, keen to distance themselves from it, declared that while 99 per cent of all motorcyclists were upstanding citizens 1 per cent were not. The Boozefighters MC were in Hollister and one of the clubs maligned by this statement. The '1%' was official.

He called it Mariah, after the wind. Custom parts were few and far between but the earliest styles had been established having appeared in bobbers and race bikes of the Forties and Fifties. These early modified bikes coined the terminology and helped define certain parts such as fatbob tanks. A bobber was a cut-down Harley but a fatbob

was a cut-down Harley that retained the stock two-piece tanks that the Motor Company had used from 1936 onward. Frame mods started after the war in the manner of pre-war Hillclimb frame mods and apehanger handlebars were made from crash bars. "Before hardly anybody except Harley made handlebars, we took Harley

Below: *Curved footboards are stock Harley parts as is the foot pedal designed for heel and toe operation of the clutch. It is seen here in the engaged position but when depressed forward will remain disengaged to allow the rider to put his feet down while stationary. Foot clutches without this facility are known as 'suicide clutches'.*

crash bars – because they were so damned tough and we didn't want them on the bikes anyway -- and reshaped them. That's where the first hooks – you know out, way up in the air, and down, apehangers they call them now – came from," according to 'Wino' Willie Forkner quoted from the same 1986 interview. Other Custom parts came from the K-model introduced in 1952 such as the solo seat and the Sportster introduced as the XL in 1957. The Sportster tank became a perennial favorite. The rear fender was still

Left: *This Knucklehead chopper from Texas uses cast VL spring legs.*
Right: *After the Fifties' introduction of the K-model Harley, small solo seats and Sportster gas tanks became popular on choppers.*
Below: *This Knuckle chop features belt primary drive as well as hand clutch and foot shift arrangements.*

a front fender cut down. The reason that a front one was used was because it had no hinge but followed the correct radius for the diameter of the wheel. Another trick was to use the more minimal fenders off a British bike – especially the ribbed ones – which made the big twins look more sleek.

One of the few companies in existence that did make what can be termed 'custom parts' was the one which was started by Lucile and Earl Flanders. Earl was a regular motorcycle competition rider who after the war started making custom handlebars for other competitors. He bent the tube to suit his customers' requirements and manufactured them to specific widths. Another product which still bears his name are Flanders

Below: *Piratical skull emblems have long been popular on choppers as this hand shift lever on a Fifties' bobber shows. The flame paint-job has its roots in post-war years to indicate that this is a hot bike and to imply motion.*

risers – sometimes known as 'dog bones' because of their shape – which are a pair of extension bars to lift the handlebars above the stock handlebar clamp.

Stroker motors became popular when mechanics started discovering that through mixing and matching of Harley engine components it was possible to increase the capacity of a twin. One method of achieving this was to use the crank pin, flywheels and con rods out of the VL flathead and incorporate them into the later engines. The VL had a longer stroke than the overhead-valve engines and when used with the standard bore pistons increased the displacement without having to resort to expensive machining. The nickname of 'Stroker' is self-explanatory since capacity was increased by increasing the stroke.

Something happened in March 1948 that would later propel the chopper far beyond California's freeways. The first chapter of the Hells Angels was founded in Berdoo –

Right: *The Hydra-Glide with its rigid frame and telescopic forks set the style for later choppers because of its functional elegance.*
Below right: *Martin Henderson's bobber has cut-down fenders but the wide stock gas tank so would have been called a fatbob.*

San Bernardino, California. By 1954 the club was becoming established in Frisco – San Francisco, California. It is recorded that in order to found another chapter a rider known as Rocky traveled north on a classic chopper of the time. The machine featured tall apehanger bars as well as chromed XA springer forks. The latter components were the forks from an experimental World War II Harley–Davidson and were four inches longer than stock springers. The cast VL springers off pre-war big twin flatheads were equally desirable for early choppers for similar reasons. The mix-and-match concept of the chopper was firmly established at the very beginning.

1947 Knucklehead

This bike, one of the last Knuckleheads, was photographed in Daytona in 1997 and is typical of early choppers and correct in every detail even as far as the owner-made apehangers. These were carefully constructed by sweating the original handlebars out of the fork clamp and fitting new tubes before chroming.

Specification

Owner: Dan Hawkins
City: Langhorne, Pennsylvania

General

Year: 1947
Make & model: HD FL
Built: Owned 20 years
Assembly: Owner
Time: Many hours

Engine

Year: 1947
Model: FL Knucklehead
Rebuilder: Owner
Displacement: 74cu. in.
Modifications: Magneto ignition
Air cleaner: Dixie Manufacturing
Pipes: Upswept fishtails

Transmission

Type: Four-speed
Year: 1947
Modifications: None
Shifting: Jockey shift

Finish

Paint: Phil Jardwa
Color: Purple
Special paint: Flawless

Frame

Type: Rigid
Year: 1947
Builder: HD
Rake: Stock
Stretch: Stock
Other modifications: Toolbox bracket removed

Accessories

Bars: Apehangers
Risers: None

Fenders

Front: None
Rear: Bobbed dresser

Headlight: Bates
Tail light: Sparto
Speedo: Tank mounted dash
Seat: Solo saddle
Front pegs: HD footboards
Rear pegs: None
Electrics: 12 volts
Gas tank: Stock HD
Oil tank: Stock HD
Primary cover: Stock HD
Sissy bar: None
Mirrors: None

Forks

Type: HD springers
Extension: None
Builder: HD
Special features: Chromed

Wheels

Front: Laced
Size: 21in
Hub: Star
Brake: Drum
Rear: Laced
Size: 16in
Hub: Star
Brake: Drum

1960–1969

PSYCHEDELIC CYCLES

THE CHOPPER EVOLVED from the race-influenced bobber into the apehangered chopper in an imprecise way. It wasn't as if the clock simply stopped on one style then started for another. Styles simply metamorphosed from one thing to another in the manner of a kaleidoscope and given the counter-culture, the summer of love and the psychedelic times that the Sixties were reputed to be, it's an appropriate analogy. George Wethern documented the early Sixties in his 1979 book, *Wayward Angel:*

'In 1960, there were relatively few custom shops where dollars could be swapped for a sleek, chrome stallion. Grooming one yourself was the surest way to get a worthy mount.' He went on to describe the process:

Left: *This Sixties-style chopper is based around a 1947 EL Knucklehead engine and frame. The gas tank is from a British bike.*
Below: *Owner Lawrence Poole says that "the bike represents a different America to that you see today" and likes it all the more for that.*

'In addition to about $3000 you needed mechanical know-how and energy to break down and refine a seventy-four-cubic-inch Harley–Davidson that rolled from the factory with donut tires, a bulbous gas tank, heavy fenders and vanity size mirrors and an uninspiring paintjob. We called them garbage wagons, but the 700 pound Harley stockers rolled like two-wheeled Cadillacs.' It was clear that a stock Harley was regarded only as the raw material from which a chopper would emerge. 'Behind the piggish pro-

file was amazing power waiting to be freed with welding torches, wrenches and screwdrivers. With the cycle stripped to the bare frame, the engine was torn down, bored out to 80 cubic inches, pumped up in horsepower. A bicycle-sized twenty-one inch front wheel was fitted to extended front forks that raked back the cut-down frame, the effect multiplied by riser handlebars with silver dollar sized mirrors. The fenders were thrown away or bobbed to the legal minimum. The cushy banana seat was thrown away and replaced with a lean saddle, the gas tank exchanged for a stinger with a twelve coat finish of lacquer. Finally, chrome pipes snorting, the beast stood ready to buck with a chomp of metal gears.' The finished bike was acknowledged as being 200lb lighter and therefore faster because of both the improved power-to-weight ratio and the tuned engine.

Freewheeling Frank, writing of the same

era in 1967, defined a chopper in much the same vein and also noted its origins as the particular choice of the '1%'. He wrote: 'A chopper means a Harley–Davidson motorcycle that has been stripped of extra accessories, including the fenders and tanks, which leaves only the frame and engine. These are then replaced with small fenders and one tank – along with straight pipes as the main changes. This leaves the motorcycle looking like a lean and furious monster. It's our creation, our breed of horse. We love them.'

Basically from 1948 to 1965 the Panhead was boss and its top end clatter a familiar

Below: *The British gas tank has been sculptured using steel and bondo, as has the rear fender. The sissy bar is adorned and the paintwork is ornate. This shows the transition from straight bobbers to bikes which have been both chopped and refinished to a specific style.*

and beloved sound. The big V-twin motor looked at its best in a hardtail frame (i.e. Harley frames that pre-date the introduction of the Duo-Glide). The looks of a rigid and a V-twin started it all. The only suspension was the ten-pound rear tire pressure but the style was low, lean and clean. A righteous ride of the time consisted of the major components from the 74cu. in. (1200cc) Harley–Davidson 'hog' and as little else as possible. Chopped hogs were little more than the heavy Harley frame, forks and wheels, a 74 cu. in. V-twin engine, small gas tank and tiny seat. Much more recently Harley–Davidson registered the word HOG as an acronym for the Harley Owners Group. They then set about litigating against all the chopper shops that had been using this particular slang in their shop names for decades. The irony in this is that the company has regularly distanced itself from the '1%' and their choppers but frequently takes

aspects of their style for its own, even admitting to the notoriety of the past in advertising copy and equipping HOG members with back patches.

The increasing numbers of British bikes being imported into the USA meant that it was necessary to strip a Harley of its surplus parts as well as fitting dirt-track type components and tuning the V-twin. This meant that the Harley could be made to run on equal terms with the lighter British machines whether it was on the track or from stop light to stop light. Harley's XL Sportsters were intended to compete with the British imports. However, by the mid-Sixties the

Right: *The peanut tank is British, and the ape-hangers and Bates headlamp are typical chop.*
Below: *Innovation in early choppers took the form of modified shifters and linkages in this case a bayonet handle and chrome chain respectively. The pedal set-up is a 'suicide clutch'.*

chopper had gone far beyond a stripped-down hog – it was rapidly becoming a work of art. The original idea of making modifications to improve the motorcycle's function were overtaken by those to drastically change its form. Apehanger bars, bobbed fenders, small gas tanks and tiny seats were still *de rigueur* but tall sissy bars, mini dual

headlights, skinny front wheels, long mufflers that sometimes extended up the side of the sissy bar and other such custom touches were becoming more and more common. Chrome parts and custom painted gas tanks were also becoming increasingly popular. Sissy bars, so named because they stopped a pillion passenger from falling off the rear of

Below: *Dale Richardson in Severance, Colorado, aboard the late Sixties' Knuckle-head machine which he painstakingly restored to its former glory as a chopper rather than as a stock bike.*
Right: *When restoring it, Dale replaced missing parts with those in the right style: old-time saddlebags, a sissy bar and a stepped seat.*

the machine, frequently reached to head height and were adorned with bayonets, swastikas or sculptured bar designs as well as acting as a place to mount the tail light and license plate. In some places – and particularly in Texas – they are referred to as 'bitch bars'.

The Sixties, for right or wrong, were the era of LSD and free love, of beautiful people and hippies, of Alan Ginsberg and Ken Kesey, of the Vietnam War – the US Marine Corps deployed in South Vietnam in 1965 as the USA assumed a full combat role in South

East Asia – and the protests against it. The late Sixties saw America bitterly divided over the issues surrounding the Vietnam War. The belief that bikers and Hells Angels were the defenders of the counter-culture and the flower people's guardians had been

Below: *This chop features genuine Harley springers that had been considerably extended before being chromed. Wide dresser-type bars are an alternative to apehangers. Headlamp and horn are in original positions.*
Right: *Dale and Martha on board.*

exposed as a myth in the same year. A notable moment had been when the Oakland Hells Angels had interrupted an anti-war protest march from radical Berkeley toward the Army Depot in Oakland. The truth of the situation was that in the main bikers tended to be blue collar in upbringing and outlook while the radical liberals were middle class.

It was inevitable that the bikes of the Sixties would reflect the psychedelic times in

which they were constructed. Esoteric paint jobs and ever longer forks became the norm and a definite style evolved. A radical chopper of the time featured a rigid frame, long forks – as often as not chromed springers – pullback bars, a sissy bar and a multi-hued paintjob of swirls and shapes. To incorporate the extended forks the frame rake needed to be altered.

Alteration of the neck rake can have serious consequences for the handling characteristics of a motorcycle and was the subject of enormous scrutiny. It is almost impossible to generalize about alterations to the rake of a motorcycle front fork assembly but it is an important question for the builders and riders of choppers and those who regulate their construction and use. The two broad areas that need to be considered are handling and structure. Considering the latter first, the structure question concerns whether the frame of the motorcycle is stiff enough for the forces exerted by any front fork assembly. The longer forks exert different stresses on a frame. Whether a frame is adequate depends on the forces applied to the structure, the size and shape of the frame, and the materials from which it is assembled. All the forces applied to the forks and frame neck result from forces applied

Left: *The bars are mounted on 'dog bone' risers, described thus because of their resemblance to the dog bones seen in cartoons. They clamp around the bars and around a custom top yoke for the springer forks. The bicycle bell is typical chopper humor.*

Above: *The headstock of the frame has been raked to suit the forks which are typical of old-style custom dual seats. This chopper features a piece of a Lone Star beer can around its ignition coil because it was originally built in Texas.*

originally at the front wheel, be they constant or varying. (Constant forces are those such as weight of the machine while varying ones are those generated by braking and turning.) Lengthening forks without physically altering the neck rake of the frame still alters the rake because of the additional length in the forks. It also changes the weight distribution of the whole motorcycle to the wheels – the longer the forks the less weight is supported by the front wheel, i.e. the constant load is reduced, although the center of gravity stays almost constant in relation to the rear wheel. Altering the neck rake of the motorcycle frame has similar effects and, of course, the steering neck loads vary with wheelbase because of the torque applied. The load on the front wheel decreases as the load on the frame neck increases due to the fact that the lever increases faster than the weight decreases as wheelbase is lengthened. When the motorcycle is moving the forces applied to the front wheel increase rapidly when the wheel rolls over bumps. The forces applied vary both in terms of amount of force applied and also the direction from which it is applied,

including cornering and braking forces. The rule of thumb is that cornering forces when the machine is banked over to 45° will increase the weight of bike and rider by around 40 per cent. The neck torque will also be raised by 40 per cent independent of neck rake and extension. Braking loads are more dependent on wheelbase, in turn dependent on both neck rake and extension.

Braking with the rear wheel only some distance behind the center of gravity gives rise to a torque action that results in an increased force on the front wheel and as the weight of the whole does not increase there is less weight on the rear wheel. If the brakes are applied harder, the weight on the front wheel increases further and the weight on the rear decreases correspondingly. The next stage is that any further increase in torque through yet harder braking will cause the wheel to skid. When only one wheel is braked the torque caused will be less than when both are braked so the weight shift will be correspondingly less as will braking force. The actual percentages are affected by wheelbase. For example, with an 85 inch wheelbase almost 60 per cent of the braking force of a two-wheel system can be achieved with only the rear brake while on a machine with a stock wheelbase the percentage is considerably smaller. Structurally the percentage of torque increase on the steering neck is most important and in rear brake-only machines the percentage increase is dependent on wheelbase but when both brakes are used it is almost 60 per cent constantly. These figures mean that particularly long wheelbase choppers with front and rear brakes needed frame necks up to 90 per cent stronger than stock, and rear brake-only bikes (which were, and are, not legal everywhere) needed frame necks up to 70 per cent stronger than stock.

Loads that affect the steering neck must be transmitted to it by the forks and have a force-versus-compression characteristic inbuilt. In the case of springer and girder forks there is some kind of damping through either friction or viscous damping. Even the friction in the swiveling joints has some damping effect but the front end needs to be constructed so that the springs are not bottomed out when the machine is static. The dynamic loading of the forks varies depending on the direction from which the load is applied, something affected by rake, the size of bump and the speed at which it is hit.

Handling at various speeds is influenced by length of wheelbase as well as rake and trail. Rake is as described above and trail is the distance from an imaginary line down from the center of the axle to where it intersects with an imaginary line down from the steering neck at the angle of the neck. A bike with a short wheelbase, short forks, small rake angle and correspondingly small trail will handle well at low speeds and be maneuverable, which makes them ideal, for example, for cross-country, off-road bikes, while a longer wheelbase, bigger rake and therefore larger trail will be more stable at higher speeds. Drag bikes are an example of this extreme; road bikes, race bikes and similar fit somewhere in between. In choppers the style is more important than the function although the machine has to be rideable. As

Right: Easyriders *magazine had replicas of the* Easy Rider *film choppers built for promotional purposes. This is Peter Fonda's Captain America Panhead chopper.*

a result many choppers are stable and comfortable at freeway speeds but less stable and maneuverable at low speeds. Adjusting the angle of the steering neck is one way to account for all these factors and to accommodate longer forks. In the late Sixties a frame modification known as a gooseneck became popular. It was so-called because the finished frame resembled a goose's neck. The frame top tube to the headstock was extended forward and the downtube was extended up and forward before the steering neck was refitted. This had the effect of lengthening the wheelbase and adjusting the

Left: *The Panhead engine in the replica is almost entirely polished or plated as in the oil tank and frame. It was photographed in Daytona in 1997.*
Below: *The Mustang tank features the famous 'Stars-and-Stripes' paintjob that has been much used over the years. The altered headstock angle to suit the overlong forks is clearly seen.*

neck to suit extended or aftermarket forks. Springer forks were popular initially for choppers and as aftermarket forks became commonly manufactured the problems with excessive trail could be eliminated through use of different length of rockers, i.e. the plates that connect both pairs of legs of the forks and carry the front axle. The conclusions that chopper builders soon came to were that frame necks required considerable strengthening for all but very small increases in wheelbase, rake and trail alterations could be mastered, and that as braking forces are not concentrated in the front wheel in long wheelbase bikes they were not as unmanageable or unsafe as some over-zealous traffic cops might claim.

Numerous custom parts and chopper parts companies started in business in the late Sixties including two Minnesota companies: Smith Brothers and Fetrow of Minneapolis, and Drag Specialties of Eden Prairie. In 1969 Chicago Cycle Specialties of

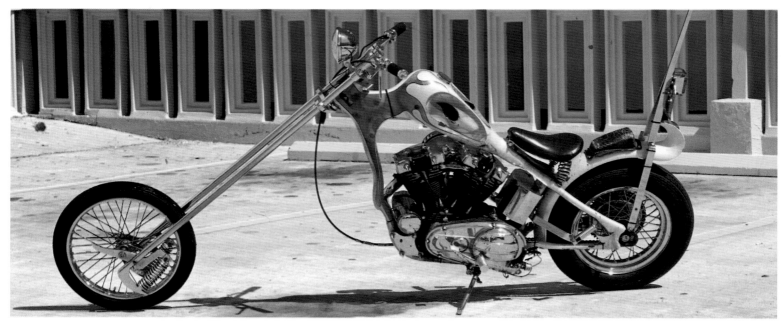

2521 North Cicero Avenue, Chicago, were advertising tubular gas and oil tanks, fork tube extensions, custom handlebars, seats, fenders and custom upswept exhausts. For 'show or go' there were pipes listed for 1947 and earlier ohv, 1948 and later ohv, 1958 ohv suspension frames (Knuckles, Pans and Duo-Glides) and XLCH Sportsters. Apart from those for the Duo-Glide, they retailed at $49 and extended way above the rider's head.

Possibly the biggest boost choppers have

Above left: *This 1959 Sportster chop belongs to Eric Love from Georgia. It is an original unrestored late-Sixties' chopper with a heavily-moulded frame and tank and tall sissy bar.*
Below left: *The tiny gas tank is sculptured and incorporates decorative vents. The moulding is cracking from the vibrations of 30 years but the recent owner plans to put that right.*

ever had came in the last year of the decade. Columbia Pictures released *Easy Rider*. This film more than anything else propelled the image of the chopper and the biker beyond the boundaries of California and its outlaw clubs and San Francisco's Haight-Ashbury circles. However, it wasn't the first of the biker movies. Kramer's *The Wild One* had that distinction and there had been others through the Sixties including *Wild Angels* and *Hells Angels '69* and *Hells Angels on Wheels* which had starred Jack Nicholson. *Easy Rider* was not a big budget movie; it had cost only $375,000 to make and would go on to eventually gross more than $20 million for its distributors. It didn't have a complex plot, simply following Wyatt and Billy on their choppers and on the road, but it captured the mood, moment and the movement of the time perfectly. Hells Angel Maz

Harris writing in 1985 recalled his visit to the cinema when the film was initially screened: 'It was like drifting off into another world, a world which we desperately wished to experience for ourselves. In that single ninety-four minute, budget movie, Dennis Hopper managed to encapsulate brilliantly the very spirit of freedom that we had all felt, at one time or another, out there on the road. He presented on screen a ceremonial vindication of what we'd known

Below: *The front end is of an unusual custom design which features some suspension that works on the same principle as girder forks, in that bumps are absorbed by the springs that control the movement of the rocker (connected to the axle) in relation to the forks connected to the frame via the headstock and bearings. No front brake is fitted.*

all along but were unable to articulate.'

The film follows two enigmatic characters, Wyatt played by Peter Fonda and Billy played by Dennis Hopper, on their trip cross-country aboard two Harley choppers. The film gives no clue about their past. It's not where they've come from but where they are going to that is important. Their destination is ultimately Mardi Gras in New Orleans but it could be anywhere. They are, as the Steppenwolf theme song says: 'Looking for adventure and whatever comes our way'. The film is set in the uncertain times of the Vietnam War era. The American Army was engaged in the struggle for Hill 937 – Hamburger Hill – east of the Laotian border

Left: *Sissy bars came in many shapes and styles and frequently acted as places on which to mount the tail light and license plate, as shown on this Georgia bike.*
Below: *Radical styling is fabulous albeit quite dated in today's world.*

at the time of its release. The film underlines the conflicts within America's changing society and almost inevitably ends in tragedy. Their one and only companion on the road, George, a whiskey-drinking lawyer, played by Jack Nicholson, is murdered, as later are Wyatt and Billy. The tragic ending didn't alter the effect the film had on many of those who saw it and suddenly bikers everywhere were 'looking for themselves' from the saddles of choppers. Another direct effect of the movie was that it spread the word about choppers internationally, most notably to Australia and Europe.

The film portrayed choppers completely typical of the time. Both of the characters ride Panhead choppers although they differ in style. The Captain America bike is Fonda's ride. It is a wishbone rigid-framed bike with an overstock telescopic front end. Apehanger bars are mounted on risers. There is no front brake or fender. A Mustang tank, dual seat and tall sissy bar are fitted, and the chopper

is finished with a Stars-and-Stripes flag paintjob. Hopper's ride is a flamed chop. It too features a wishbone frame and Mustang tank but the forks are not as long or as raked and have T-bars bolted to the top yoke. The bike has a small, English-style front fender and the stock drum brake. These two choppers are the machines that launched a style

Left: *The Maltese Cross was a popular configuration for both mirrors and tail lights for almost two decades. Vintage-style rubber bulb horns were also a popular accessory as were vintage-style lights front and rear.*

for choppers that irrevocably link choppers and long forks together. Fashion being what it is, while both bikes would still be welcomed at any custom bike event, Fonda's looks like a late-Sixties/early-Seventies chopper while Hopper's slightly more restrained machine hasn't really ever gone out of style with the possible exception of the style of handlebars.

So famous have these two motorcycles become that *Easyriders* magazine built replicas for display and promotional purposes – the replica Captain America bike is included in this book. As a direct result of that movie, rigid frames and high bars are as much a part of motorcycling for many as highways and Harleys.

1960s Knucklehead

This chopper was originally built back in 1969 in Texas. Dale Richardson from Greeley, Colorado, purchased it in an incomplete state and rebuilt it using parts sympathetic to its age such as a stepped dual seat, aftermarket fatbob tank and had parts rechromed and the bike freshly painted in a way that has its inspiration in the Captain America Panhead from the same era.

Specification

Owner: Dale Richardson
City: Greeley, Colorado

General

Year: 1947
Make & model: HD FL
Built: 1969
Assembly: Rebuilt in 1995 by owner
Time: 6 months

Engine

Year: 1947
Model: Knucklehead
Rebuilder: Owner
Displacement: 74cu. in.
Modifications: Chrome parts
Air cleaner: HD circular
Pipes: Slash cut drag

Transmission

Type: Four-speed
Year: 1947
Modifications: None
Shifting: Foot

Finish

Paint: Steve Peif
Color: Red, white and blue
Special paint: Stars-and-Stripes

Frame

Type: HD Rigid
Year: 1947
Builder: HD
Rake: Increased from stock
Stretch: None
Other modifications: None

Accessories

Bars: Dresser
Risers: Dog bone

Fenders

Front: None
Rear: Flat bobbed

Headlight: Bates
Tail light: Catseye
Speedo: Tank mounted dash
Seat: Custom stepped dual
Front pegs: Footboards
Rear pegs: Gynaecological
Electrics: 12 volts
Gas tank: Aftermarket fatbob
Oil tank: Chromed horseshoe
Primary cover: HD
Sissy bar: Low rise
Mirrors: Custom

Forks

Type: Springer
Extension: 6in overstock
Builder: HD
Special features: Originally extended in '69

Wheels

Front: Laced
Size: 21in
Hub: HD Star
Brake: None
Rear: Laced
Size: 16in
Hub: HD Star
Brake: Drum

1970–1979

CHANGING TIMES

THE CHOPPER WAS acknowledged as existing by Harley–Davidson in 1970. In that year The Motor Company launched the Super Glide. *Cycle* magazine put it on the cover of their November 1970 issue and inside the magazine said: 'The members of the Harley–Davidson styling team, in response to the genius of Dick Hirschberg, the impact of the chopper phenomenon, and the success of *Easy Rider*, have savaged the venerable Electra-Glide like tigers at a goat and herewith present to you the...Super

Glide, Sonnet on Extravagance.' What had brought this machine from a Milwaukee drawing board and onto the street? According to *Cycle,* who had asked William G. Davidson, HD's styling chief, it was 'the

Left: *This Sportster shows the scale of the Seventies' custom aftermarket. The frame, rear wheel, fender, pillion pegs, sissy bar and seat are all custom parts.*
Below: *The front also features custom gas tank, forks, speedo and handlebars.*

influence of the California bob-jobs; not full choppers as such, but lightened, leaned-down bikes that were recognizable as 74s.' The Super Glide was launched with a Red, White and Blue paintjob but, despite the very evident parallel with Fonda's ride in *Easy Rider*, the manufacturer was keen to distance itself from the whole chopper scene. Davidson had this to say: 'As a company we're leery of the chopper image and any kind of extremism.'

It was an uncertain period for the Red,

White and Blue then because times were changing quickly. President Nixon had been inaugurated in 1969 and had taken a completely different approach to the Vietnam War. His scaling down of US Military involvement was one aspect of this. Despite the ongoing controversy about the Vietnam War, some dealers clearly knew who bought the Harleys they sold; the 1970 adverts for Dudley Perkins Co., a San Francisco dealer since 1914, included a line that read 'Returning Servicemen Welcome'.

Harley–Davidson had introduced their refined overhead-valve 74 cubic inch engine in 1966 and it quickly became known as the Shovelhead because of the resemblance of the rocker covers to the backs of upturned shovels. It may seem contrived but as a nickname it is now universal. This engine was used in the Super Glide which was without doubt the factory's interpretation of a custom bike. Harley had taken an FL Electra-Glide, removed the cumbersome front end and replaced it with the lighter one from an

Below: *One of the Seventies' styles which became enormously popular was the long, low chopper. This Sportster chop has been built along those lines using a stretched rigid frame with the headstock reworked to allow the fitting of overstock length girder forks. The wheels are 21 and 16 inch diameter front and rear respectively.*

XL Sportster hence its FX designation. They had fitted a 3.5 gallon fatbob tank and a custom-styled dual seat unit with an integral frenched tail light. Amid talk of the lack of frame flex, of rake and trail and cornering, *Cycle* magazine said: 'Everybody likes it; everybody has to like it for one reason or another.'. They went on to predict that the Super Glide would succeed like no other motorcycle the company had ever built. The magazine was right. The Super Glide has been in Harley's range ever since and the concept of the factory custom motorcycle was proven beyond all doubt. Subsequently, most of the world's major motorcycle manufacturers have at one time or another included factory customs in their range.

In the same issue of *Cycle* magazine that tested the new Super Glide, Routt's Cycle Center Inc., of Hyattsville, Maryland, were advertising extended forks, fork braces, bolt-on rigid rear frame sections and custom seats. With the exception of the forks, all were advertised for British bikes and Harleys, the fork tubes were also available for Hondas. The Seventies would see a burgeoning market for choppers powered by engines other than those of Harley–Davidson manufacture. This was partially because of the availability and cheapness of

Above: *Pig Pen has been riding this radical Seventies' Panhead chop since that decade. He posed for this picture in Steamboat Springs, Colorado, in the fall of 1996, a favorite place of his and one he has passsed through for many years.*

these other makes of motorcycle, especially those from British and Japanese manufacturers. Despite this, many of the so-called custom components used in their construction owed their origin to Harley–Davidson; fatbob and Sportster tanks are obvious examples, as well as springer forks and rigid frames the like of which had never been used by Honda, as well as specific items such as tombstone tail lights which were stock Harley items between 1946 and 1954. It is equally true to say that Maltese Cross tail lights, prism tanks and tall sissy bars are custom items designed specifically for choppers, regardless of their engine type. The tradition of building choppers powered by engines other than Harleys endures; in Great Britain there is a long tradition of building 'specials' which started with café racer Tritons – a combination of Norton cycle parts and a Triumph Twin engine. In Europe, Harley–Davidsons were not at all plentiful with the exception of military surplus WLA and

Above: *The plunger frame had been used by major makers over the years until superseded by the swinging arm rear suspension. It made a comeback during the Seventies for choppers because it offered some suspension and yet still retained most of the looks of a hardtail.*

WLC models, so in the early Seventies European choppers were frequently based around these as well as various British and Japanese bikes. The Triumph twin and Honda Four engines were both popular choices.

In 1972 chopper parts were being advertised by a number of California companies including D&D Distributors of Burbank, Eyeball Engineering of Rialto, Mother's Choppers of Anaheim, Paughco of North Hollywood, Durfee of Stanton, and Vista Chopper Products of Glendale. Of these, D&D, Eyeball, Mother's, Durfee and Paughco offered long front ends alongside other products. There were many more around the US in business or about to be: Arlen Ness, Gary Bang, Denver's Choppers,

Left: *This Seventies' Sportster chop features a Mustang tank, square-section sissy bar, and custom wheels. Wheels with a minimal number of square-section tubular spokes became popular in the Seventies and were manufactured for both drum and disc brake fitment.*

Bay Area Custom Cycles, American Motorcycle Engineering, B.C. Choppers, C&G Manufacturing, Santee, P&P, SIE, Hallcraft, Invader, Chopper Corner, HR Custom Choppers, GME, Tom's Accessories Inc., Cycle Saloon Inc., Allied, Jardine, T&S, Pucketts, Cycles International, Hill Engineering, Ed's Chopper Parts, Cycle

Parts Unlimited, B&R products, Michigan Motorcycle Accessories, Red Rider, Expert Cycle, Cycle Seats, California Choppers, Two Wheelers, Custom Cycle Delight Inc., Forking by Frank, D&K, Cycle Supply and many more.

Parts were being designed and thought up all the time. John Flanders of the Flanders company was on the road selling handlebars to motorcycle shops when the guys at Cheat'ah Choppers of 3500 W. Westminster Boulevard in Santa Ana, California, asked for a specific design of handlebar that would bend right back. It became known as the 'California pullback' and within months became Flanders' top selling handlebar of the Seventies. There was another similar design which were referred to as 'six bend pullbacks' because the design incorporated six bends in the tubing. Such was the boom for chopper building that an Illinios-based

Left: *Custom forward controls for both rear brake and gear shift operation became popular in the Seventies and were made for most chopper applications. This chromed unit is a gear shift.*
Below: *Ornately hand-tooled leather seats were popular for custom applications and were hard wearing.*

company called SIE, who advertised as being the nation's largest distributor of custom parts and also claimed to 'ride what we sell', offered franchises to would-be chopper shop proprietors on a $2500 minimum offer.

Other custom components gained in popularity. Gas tanks shaped like small coffins, prism and also diamond-shaped ones all

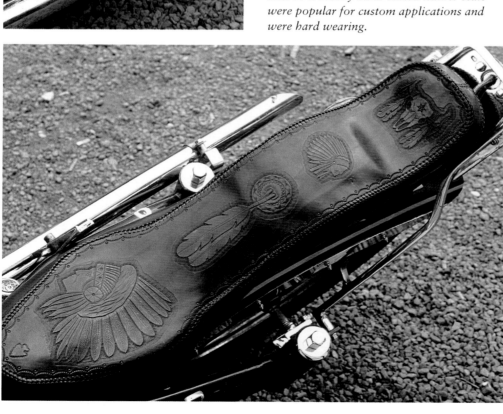

appeared in advertisements, and more importantly, on bikes. Seats soon followed the full height of sissy bars. Seats stepped by six inches or more became known as 'King and Queen' seats. In addition, disc brake conversions, plunger frames custom exhausts and hexagonal and octagonal section oil tanks were all being manufactured. 'Highway

pegs' were another custom component and allowed the rider to put his feet forward of the normal riding position and ride with legs outstretched forward on long stretches of road – hence their name. Such pegs complemented the upright riding position of the chopper as compared to a stock bike.

The style of custom paintwork progressed

Below: *This rigid-framed Ironhead chopper features a number of Seventies-style components including the six tubular steel spoke wheels and the octagonal section oil tank beneath the seat. Other components such as the fatbob tank and rear fender are popular chopper parts. The stock front end has been retained albeit with a custom front fender.*

through the Seventies too. Graphics became popular and often included panels of metalflake paint. Murals portraying any number of scenes became fashionable and were painstakingly applied by airbrush specialists. Popular themes for murals included dragons, snakes and mythical characters in fantasy scenes as well as naked and partially naked women. Perennially popular designs and variations on flames and skulls also evolved in parallel with the newer styles.

As the popularity of choppers increased

Left: *The aftermarket parts industry enabled bikers to build choppers within certain styles such as this rigid-framed big twin. Sissy bar, fender, fork tubes and primary cover are all custom items.*

Below: *Slash cut mufflers – note the angled cut ends – are one of a number of popular styles of custom exhausts.*

exponentially a number of enthusiast magazines were launched – *Choppers*, *Street Chopper* and *Custom Chopper* in 1970, and then *Easyriders* in June 1971. While several came and went, others went from strength to strength. *Easyriders* is still being published and *Street Chopper* evolved into *Hot Bike*, again still being published. The specific chopper magazines were the first regular publications to chronicle the development of ideas and trends within chopper building circles. The widespread US and international

Right: *Fletcher Thompson's Knucklehead chop had its frame headstock raked in order to accomodate the overstock fork tubes and sliders from a Hydra-Glide model.*
Below: *The stepped dual seat is a custom one which has the effect of lowering the rider into the angle between the frame and the rear fender.*

Below: *Arlen Ness was a pioneer of the long, low Bay Area Low Rider style of chopper. These three examples built by him are all based around Sportster engines. The top one has some vintage styling touches such as the early style tank and springers. The center one, 'Two Bad', is the most extreme with two engines. The bottom one has a prismatic tank.*

distribution also meant that fashions would no longer remain localized. From the pages of a magazine it was possible, by looking closely at featured bikes, reading how-to features, and by mail ordering parts from advertisers, to build a chopper almost anywhere. Yet another publication that soon became highly regarded was the *Jammer's*

Handbook. Mil Blair was the man behind D&D but later changed the company name to Jammer Cycle, and with Joe Teresi and Lou Kimzey, produced a series of *Jammer's Handbooks*. These were a combination of feature bikes, technical features and parts catalog. They contained parts for Harleys, British and Japanese bikes and were pub-

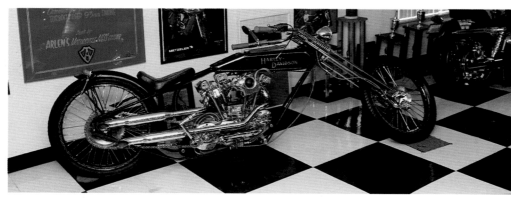

lished annually. As early as 1975 Jammer Cycle Products were able to say the following in their advertising: 'We've been around a long time – since back when chopper was a dirty word – and we plan on being around for a long time to come.' This section of an advert hints at how reviled choppers were by some people. Jammer stayed in business until 1993 and it is hard to underestimate the influence which their handbooks had on chopper builders simply through making parts available. In 1976, for example, the company reprinted their first three handbooks as one 160-page volume which listed 2000 product lines.

What is immediately evident from the

Below: *Engraving, gold plating and intricate gold leaf scroll paintwork were three finishing techniques that became popular in the Seventies. Strutted tails – substituting the rear shock absorbers with struts to make a swing arm frame into a rigid and lower the rear – was a popular styling trick, as was fitting angular paneled gas tank and fenders.*

magazines that chronicle the Seventies is that the desire to be different meant that some choppers were gaudy and featured everything to excess. In some ways they were almost a parody of the purity that had gone before. By the mid-Seventies even the psychedelic had become mainstream and many parts were being manufactured to be different for the sake of being different rather than how the finished components looked. With hindsight, other components appear ugly as a result of the manufacturing technology then available especially where new technology existed but could not be applied sufficiently well to retain the graceful lines of older style parts. However, at the time these parts were considered *avant garde*. Square section girder forks, candy twist steel springer forks, and spoked Invader wheels that were assembled with a minimal number of square section tubular spokes were all fashionable items but would now be considered dated. Many of the smaller chopper components were tacky including Maltese Cross mirrors and tail

Left: *This chop combines a 1957 rigid Harley frame and a 1974 Alternator Shovel motor into a classic chop.*
Above: *It is owned by Tig Leake from Leesburg, Florida, who built it with a Panhead engine in 1971. The front end is 15 inches over stock and in order to fit them, 6 1/2 inches have been let into the frame downtubes.*

lights as well as tall sissy bars that incorporated bayonets, swastikas or peace signs and Nazi Eagle tail lights. The fashion for swastikas and Iron Crosses came about from the 'One-Percenters' who wore World War II souvenirs as part of outlandish dress styles in order to shock the citizens, as the non-biking public were disparagingly referred to. It invariably worked, although later a few white power elements did become evident within the biker community, as they are in any other large segment of society drawn from those with varying backgrounds and outlooks.

There were, of course, many exceptions to the lack of taste in some Seventies' chopper components and it was possible to build a

righteous ride. With more than two decades of hindsight it is clear that the choppers that do not appear gaudy and tasteless – even though they are clearly dated – are those that have long flowing lines rather than clumsy angular ones. Two distinct styles evolved. As well as choppers with long forks, a long, low, super-extended bike became popular in the San Francisco Bay Area during the early Seventies. The style was developed by Arlen Ness, Ron Simms and others in Northern California and became popular all over the USA and beyond. By the mid-Seventies there were two distinct styles: the low slung look popularized by the likes of Denver's Choppers, and the Nor-Cal Frisco Ness style. The latter style was based around short front ends, diamond tanks, drag bars and strutted tails. Of these main components, diamond tanks were faceted steel gas tanks, drag bars were almost straight, and flat handlebars and strutted tails were swing arm frames with the shock absorbers replaced by chromed steel struts which effectively made them rigid. The length of the strut determined how low the bike would ride. Many of these low riders and diggers used Sportster engines because it was possible to build a slimmer bike than if the bigger 74 cubic inch Harley V-twin engine was used. Certain components were designed especially for these bikes, the hardhead frame and Bay Area springers being just two examples. The hardhead frame was a section of frame that incorporated a steering head that required welding into a stock frame and had the effect of both altering the rake and lengthening the frame. The Bay Area springers were a slender version of Harley's springer forks that

Right: *Choppers are irreverent machines and there is little more so than this portrayal of the Mona Lisa topless on a Mustang tank.*
Below: *Coffin tanks are so named because of their coffin shape. The tank, headstock, paintwork and handlebars are typical Seventies.*

when used on such a bike enhance the slim, almost delicate, lines. A third component designed for these low riders was a glass-fiber rear fender designed by Arlen Ness. It was minimal but incorporated a mounting for the rear light.

The second style of chopper from the era was the rigid framed machine with long forks, a small gas tank on the top tube, long pullback bars, possibly a tall sissy bar and stepped seat. Often on both styles the tank and frame were moulded so that angles were smoothed out with bondo and show bikes of both kinds featured sculptured components. Some components went far beyond what was at all practical. One such item was rigid forks. These were simply chromed tubes and while they made a chopper's front end look clean and uncluttered they would not have enhanced handling. The only suspension they offered was in the flexing of the tubes.

Because of the informal nature of the chopper rider's world and the casual way choppers have evolved and fashions have developed new styles, it isn't possible to pinpoint exact dates when a particular type of chopper was no longer being built. There is generally more of a gradual shift from one style to another so that, for example, the distinction between the late Sixties and early Seventies is indistinct. However it is possible to differentiate, at a glance, between bikes from opposite ends of the decade, such was the ever-evolving process. External factors, including the changing motorcycle market in

Below: *A Mustang moped. The gas tank on these machines became so popular for choppers that replicas of the tanks had to be manufactured to meet demand. With a Bates headlamp and sprung solo saddle, the Mustang was often cannabilized for chopper parts.*

the USA, were amongst the reasons for this. In 1969 there had been a considerable amount of intense negotiation and Harley–Davidson was bought by AMF – American Machine and Foundry. This group was a huge conglomerate that owned a variety of leisure and industrial companies. AMF took control of Harley–Davidson on January 7, 1969. It was not an entirely happy marriage and led to a strike over job losses, quality control problems and all the other symptoms of dissatisfied industry. Despite these problems, the early Seventies were boom years for motorcycle sales and the AMF-controlled company upped production enormously. In the long term this was to compound quality control problems but this was not immediately evident. AMF are frequently criticized for their ownership of Harley–Davidson and the way they ran things but it is now generally accepted that if

AMF had not bought Harley–Davidson in 1969 the company would not have survived. The Seventies were the era of the new generation of Japanese superbikes and AMF began to consider withdrawing from the Harley–Davidson operation. As the decade wore on the percentage share of the market enjoyed by Harley–Davidson was declining in the face of ever-increasing numbers of Oriental imports to the USA. Unreliability, caused by quality control problems, ensured that Harleys were only bought by the dedicated few and in many cases the factory bikes were seen for what they could be rather than what they were. This was compounded by the success of the factory Super Glide models which was also to have a bearing on the styles of choppers to come.

Choppers began to seriously diversify in the mid-Seventies; as well as the varying low rider and long forked styles, there was a less

Above: *The fad for custom parts led to the production of a wide range of products including tail lights such as this 'Peace' model.*
Above right: *Long-forked bikes relied more on the rear brake which meant it was possible to use a dirt-track type spool hub.*

Right: *A popular custom builder's trick was to make motorcycle parts from other items. This led to things such as pillion footpegs made from brass knuckles, as well as using bayonet handles, door knobs and brass taps for jockey shifters.*

obvious but possibly more important divergence. Show bikes were becoming less and less like rideable street bikes and ever more extravagant so a style of chopper began to emerge designed for riding. The successful formula incorporated a mixture of factory-manufactured Harley parts such as engine, transmission and maybe the forks and frame ,with a combination of custom parts from companies such as Jammer and Paughco (perhaps the tank, frame, forks and saddle). The custom bikes that were the result were usually Panhead- or Shovelhead-powered choppers using rigid or swing arm frames and telescopic or springer forks. When fin-

ished with a combination of smaller parts from either custom suppliers or OEM parts this ensured considerable diversity in the appearance and detail of finished choppers, albeit after a certain general style. In 1979, as the decade drew toward its close, Drag Specialties were supplying many of the custom components to build a chopped Harley. Their adverts claimed that they were the No. 1 motorcycle accessory leader in the world with over 9000 dealers worldwide. In the same year Jammer were offering items such as belt primary drive conversions and stamped steel custom wheels that bolted to a hub assembly. In later years this type of wheel would be machined from billet alloy. The overall style of the rideable chopper was reflected in the factory's successful Super Glide models. These in their component form, can be considered as a Shovelhead engine in a swing arm frame with a telescopic front end, minimal fenders and other

cycle parts. This combination of parts was available through use of an AMF Harley and a number of custom components. Various FX models were built and sold throughout the Seventies including the decidedly custom-looking FXS Low Rider of 1977. This machine incorporated shorter forks with greater rake, cast wheels and a fatbob gas tank. A crinkle finish black Shovelhead engine and silver painted tank and fenders completed the custom look. With ersatz choppers rolling off the factory's assembly lines and selling off the dealers' showroom floors, the chopper entered the Eighties with something of an identity crisis.

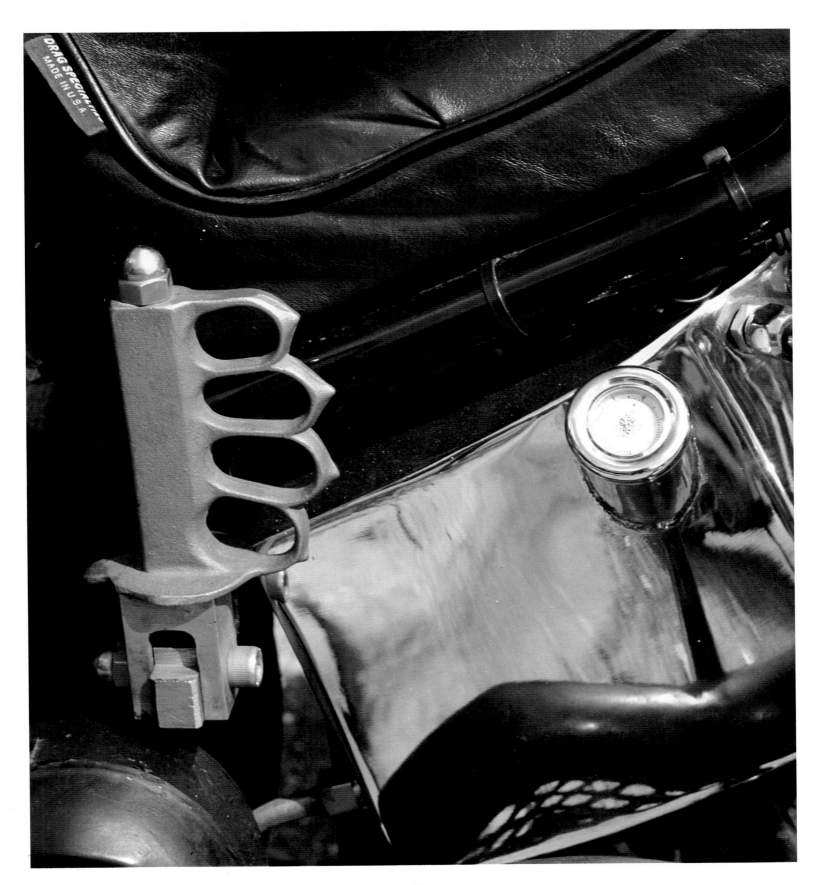

1976 Sportster

This bike is typical of the extravagant chops built in the Seventies. It features a wide range of custom parts from that time and has been finished with a paintjob typical of the day. Although it now appears gaudy it would have been a real headturner when it was first built. It has survived untouched purely by chance and been in the garage of a customer of Arlin Fatland's 2-Wheelers Motorcycle Shop in Denver since its last tag expired in 1986.

Specification

Owner: Arlin Fatland
City: Denver, Colorado

General

Year: 1976
Make & model: HD Sportster
Built: 1970s
Assembly: Unknown
Time: Unknown

Engine

Year: 1975
Model: Ironhead Sportster
Rebuilder: Unknown
Displacement: 61cu. in.
Modifications: Chromed parts
Air cleaner: Circular custom
Pipes: Two-into-one

Transmission

Type: Unit construction
Year: 1975
Modifications: None
Shifting: Foot

Finish

Paint: Custom
Color: Multi-hued
Special paint: Swirly graphics and pinstripes

Frame

Type: Plunger 'Savior' custom
Year: 1976
Builder: AMEN
Rake: As required
Stretch: As required
Other modifications: Frame chromed

Accessories

Bars: Pullback T-bars
Risers: Integral with handlebars

Fenders

Front: Mini custom
Rear: Flat

Headlight: Bates
Tail light: Knightlight
Speedo: Drag Specialties Mini
Seat: King and Queen
Front pegs: Stock
Rear pegs: AME custom
Electrics: 12 volts
Gas tank: Prismatic
Oil tank: Chromed
Primary cover: Stock HD
Sissy bar: Low rise incorporates license plate and rear light
Mirrors: Custom

Forks

Type: Custom girders
Extension: Long
Builder: Unknown
Special features: 1970s custom parts

Wheels

Front: Invader spoked
Size: 21in
Hub: Integral with wheel
Brake: Disc
Rear: Invader spoked
Size: 16in
Hub: Integral with wheel
Brake: Disc

Custom Paint by
~ BRENT~
Tampa Fla.

AGAINST THE WIND

FOR 1981, AMF Harley–Davidson took the concept of the factory custom a long way further down the chopper road; they announced the FXWG. This was an FX Super Glide with a Wide Glide front end, hence its WG suffix. It was, Harley claimed, 'the only factory built custom in sight' and featured a 21 inch front wheel, 16 inch rear, extended front forks with Electra Glide sliders, staggered short dual pipes and a bobbed rear fender. To round off the custom appearance, the FXWG was available with a flame paintjob over black or in four different metallic colors. For years Harley dealers had been helping themselves out by marketing unofficial aftermarket parts but now the factory were beginning to offer their own choppers in addition to lines of aftermarket custom parts.

There was still a market for the independent manufacturers of course despite the downturn in the US economy in the early Eighties. The aftermarket products being manufactured and distributed for Harleys and being advertised in the specialist magazines included components from Drag Specialties, Graves Plating, Performance Machine Inc., Jammer Cycle Products, Righteous Products, Brown's Plating,

Left: *For a time, much of the custom paint on was devoted to futuristic fantasy scenes.*
Below: *Denny and Priscilla Lueders with their Shovelhead chop. The headstock has been altered and the downtubes lengthened in order to fit the over stock forks.*

Left: *A rigid Shovel chop on the road at the Red River Run in New Mexico. It features 16 inch wheels at both the back and the front, and also apehangers which enhance its triangular shape.*
Below left: *Open belt primary drive conversions became popular on choppers and replaced the covered chain.*

Lonesome MFG, 2 Wheeler's M/C Shop, Paramount Speedometer, Forking by Frank, C&G Mfg Co., Paughco, Allied Distributing & Mfg. Inc., Bay Area Custom Cycles, AMEN, Phase 3, Denver's Choppers, Elite Corporation, Smith Brothers & Fetrow Inc., Custom Cycle Delight Inc., Truett & Osborn, Arlen Ness, Expert Cycle Inc., Routt's Cycle, S&S, Nostalgia Cycle, P&P Distributors, Santee, Speed & Cycle Shop Inc., Cycle Fabrications, California Cycle Works, SIE Inc., FuBaR, Chopper Specialties, Sugar

Bear's Chop Shop and, in some publications, AMF Harley–Davidson themselves. When compared to the similar list in an earlier chapter of this book (page 57), what is surprising is how many of them were in business ten years earlier.

Amongst the products they made were items upgraded to suit more modern components such as the Smith Brothers & Fetrow square section girder forks designed to accept single or twin Harley brake discs and calipers as well as the stock cast wheels. AMEN – American Motorcycle Engineering – offered the Savior frame which featured plunger-type rear suspension. This was intended to offer some rear suspension but also offer most of the looks of a rigid frame. *Street Chopper* magazine had produced a series of five builder guides to help guys get choppers up and running. They dealt with frame and tank modifications, chopper electrics, custom wheels and front ends, building your own trike, and chopper styling. Times were changing though. Gary Bang, who had been involved in the custom parts business since its earliest days, was interviewed by *Easyriders* magazine in 1987. He indicated that fashions were changing in the chopper world when he said: "We were tired of the 2.2 gallon tank, it was a style that we were tired of, absolutely tired of, just like we were tired of bell-bottom pants. Along came the gas crunch. Boy, we needed more gas. Everybody knew that. What to do? They tried making the tank bigger, but it got uglier. Then they said: "Let's put fatbobs back on." We took fatbobs off in the Sixties and threw them in the trash and now those same fatbob tanks, speedos and dashes are worth $250 a unit. So we did the fatbobs. But when we did them the front ends came lower, 'cause the tanks didn't look right up there. More fenders were put back on; it became popular to run brakes. We're talking about the style changing over eight years. Now, everybody's ready for the motorcycle they tore apart 20 years ago."

Right: *A shop called Knucklehead North built this early-Eighties style rigid chop around a 1976 74 cubic inch Shovelhead motor and a Harley rigid frame. Alloy Harley wheels appeared on chops soon after they were first used on factory bikes.*

Left and below left: *These two Eighties' rigid chops are based around rigid frames, Harley engines – Shovelhead (top), Knucklehead (bottom) – and have little in common in terms of components with the exception of the seats but despite this there is a distinct similarity in their overall shape, so established has this style of chopper become.*

Bang was also aware of the stigma of stereotyping bikers as bad guys, about which he had this to say: "Bikers are like the old cowboys. Remember the old days? The cowboys would come galloping into town and they were rough-and-ready guys. And some of those guys were real honest. Real honest, think about that. Some of them wouldn't take a nickel off a guy if he was passed out drunk. But they'd come rolling into town and they loved to drink and yell and chase women. They had good fun – rollicking jolly good fun. Those guys became obsolete. They'd come to town and have too much fun, they'd scare the s--- out of the straight people. We ain't no different from the cowboys – they did it a hundred years ago. The girls would be in the saloons just like they are today."

There were problems at Daytona and Sturgis in the early Eighties when the free-wheeling chopper lifestyle repeatedly brought the scooter tramps into conflict with authority. To the tramps sliding through the scene it all seemed trivial stuff – drinking on the street, public nudity, no rear-view mirror, apehangers too high, exhaust pipes too loud – but it meant fines and nights in the cells. Despite this the chopper guys weren't going away, they were here to stay. "When was the last time you saw a beatnik? Or better yet, a hippie? Where are the people who screamed 'freedom' in the Sixties and Seventies? Outlaw bikers were an important part of the culture of the Sixties and Seventies. And now in the Eighties, out of all the craziness of the last twenty years, only the [motorcycle] brotherhood has survived."

Right: *The Knucklehead engine was Harley–Davidson's first overhead-valve engine and because of this it has always been a favorite with chopper builders. Terry Sweeney used this one in his chopper built in a custom rigid frame.*

wrote Peter Boyles in *Denver Magazine* during 1982. While he asked a valid question in the light of drastically changing times, the question also illustrated the strength of the biker scene. In a little over thirty years it had become a solid and constant part of the general run of things. As AMF's market share declined only this one large group of riders –

hardcore bikers – stuck religiously with Harley–Davidson products. After the fad for Japanese-powered choppers passed and the fickle had gone on to other pastimes, the hardcore kept the concept of the chopper, and indeed the Harley rider, alive. In the manner of popular outlaws, this group displayed a defiant attitude to society in general.

CHOPPED HARLEYS

The attitude is succinctly summed up in J.F. Freedman's novel, *Against the Wind*, 'Some of the boys mosey over and start talking bikes (which means Harleys, of course, none of this riceburner s---). Panheads and Knuckles and suicide shifters and if you never rode an old Indian, man, you don't know what it is to get your kidneys scrambled permanent, and then some of the ladies start hovering (all the world knows ladies love outlaws)...straight society can't handle the truth they lay on the world so they've got to cut them down, categorize them, call them outlaws. Anyway so what if they are outlaws, that's the American way...' (this is Lone Wolf, the leader of the bikers, talking).

The novel is about members of the Scorpions MC but the attitude illustrated goes far beyond a single club or a single novel. The book goes on: 'F--- riceburners, f--- all foreign bikes; a real biker, and most definitely any outlaw biker, whatever colors he wears, rides a Harley. It's part of the unwritten law; you buy American and you

Right: *The Shovel engine is fitted to a rigid Santee frame with a flat fender and fatbob tank. The long front end features flat bars on risers and a brakeless spool hub. Braking is by means of a rear disc.*
Below: *Bob Kersulov's chopper is typical of many specially-constructed machines and features a 96 cubic inch engine.*

ride American. No draft-dodging pussies here, either.' So it was, the American biker rode a Harley – union-made on American soil – and was a proud patriot. They didn't start that crazy Asian war but had proudly stood and faced Charlie behind an M16 and Old Glory at Khe Sahn and all the other hell holes because freedom ain't free. The bewilderment of a working man – bikers are predominantly working class – seeing his class and kin unemployed when the country was spending its dollars on ever-increasing numbers of imports led to the bumper stickers and T-shirts that read: 'Hungry? Out of work? Eat your riceburner.' and also 'Buy American-made – the job you save might be your own.' Despite such laudable sentiments, bikers found themselves alienated by straight American society, ironically excommunicated by the citizens of the country of which they were so proud. Perceived as crude, rude and unrefined, they were considered beyond the pale by many and frequently treated as second class citizens. Such treatment came in many forms, from being refused service in bars and restaurants while on the road, being subjected to more than their fair share of attention from traffic cops, having club runs stopped at roadblocks, and having constitutional rights infringed. Hardcore bikers saw it as the price to pay for living differently – hey, bikers have more fun than people.

Led by Vaughan Beals, who had joined Harley–Davidson in 1975 in the position of a Vice-President, a group of thirteen Harley–Davidson executives raised $100 million and bought the company from AMF in 1981. The factory's advertising of the time was boosted by evocative lines such as 'The eagle soars alone'. *Easyriders* magazine reported in April 1982 that 'Harley currently sells only 31 per cent of bikes in the over 1000cc market. Honda has a 26 per cent share, Kawasaki has 16 per cent and the other Japanese manufacturers are coming on like Yamamoto at Pearl Harbor.' Vaughan Beals was interviewed on the reasons for AMF wanting to part with Harley–Davidson and was was quoted as saying: "Aggression is the key word in this industry, without it you lose your market and AMF had lost the will to fight for Harley–Davidson's share of the market." According to Beals, AMF had spent vast sums on plant building and modernization after buying Harley–Davidson but had decided it was not going to pump any more money into the firm. "It had to justify Harley–Davidson's expenses against those of its 30 or 40 other businesses," Beals recalled, "but those of us who were running AMF's motorcycle products group had to justify what was right for Harley against what was right for AMF. It was a stand-off." He also added that: "AMF considered our offer as a sort of last resort."

Soar alone though the eagle did, it flew in stormy skies. Between 1980 and 1982 Harley–Davidson had to lay off a portion of its workforce and the management appealed to the government to increase tariffs on imported Japanese motorcycles of over 700cc displacement. Harley–Davidson felt that heavyweight garbage wagons from Japan, such as the Honda Goldwing, were their main threat. The US government under the presidency of Ronald Reagan imposed tariffs of up to 50 per cent on such imports

Left: *Bill Osborn's chopper is based around a 1979 Shovelhead motor and frame.*
Right: *A neat ride depends on the details – the license plate and tombstone tail light sit neatly behind the seat.*
Below: *The frame has been modified with the fitting of a Jammer weld-on hardtail to which is fitted a flat rear guard.*

and Reagan himself went as far as visiting one of Harley–Davidson's plants. Better days were around the corner for the company and in 1983 another new engine was announced, which was officially designated the Evolution. The Evolution engine was to be Harley–Davidson's salvation and by 1984 motorcycle magazines were in a position to report that Harley–Davidson's laid-off workers had been re-employed, its market share had increased, and that the company had made a profit for the first time in three years. Vaughan Beals of Harley–Davidson was quoted as saying: "We are not out of the woods yet but we're working hard to get there. We have an obligation to the American people and the government to take advantage of the breathing room the tariffs provide. We intend to fulfil that obligation by finishing up the job at hand." One way

Right: *Arlen Ness built this radical Low Rider in the mid-Eighties. It uses a 1980 FX Shovelhead engine and transmission. The frame was specially fabricated by Jim Davis. The gold leaf paintwork and striping was done by Jeff McCann.*
Below: *The louvred rear fender and trick fender struts were all fabricated by Ness.*

Left: *The performance aspect of the Low Rider has been enhanced through the fitment of a plated and polished Magnuson supercharger with twin Rivera-modified SU carburetors.*
Above: *The frame top tube acts as a gas tank, and the bikini fairing was made by Arlen Ness.*

they went about this was by aggressively marketing the new engine: the Evolution. It was a name that was entirely appropriate, as the bottom end of the 80 cubic inch (1340cc) engine could trace its origins back through the Shovelhead and Panhead to the original 61E Knucklehead of 1936. This engine was the one major factor above all else that saved Harley–Davidson from going out of business, turning them again into a major force in the ranks of the world's motorcycle producers. Suddenly everyone, it would seem, would want a Harley.

While the Milwaukee factory was perfecting its Evolution engine, chopper building continued in the garages and backyards of bikers around the world. The dominant style was still the various permutations of the styling of the FX Super Glide. The major components were still rigid and swing arm frames, telescopic and spring front ends and Panhead and Shovelhead motors. The process of chopper building is not without its difficulties, something noted by Daniel Wolf who wrote: 'Chopping is the last stage and the ultimate challenge in personalizing a motorcycle. The biker not only rebuilds the entire machine, he virtually redesigns it. When a biker spends a couple of thousand dollars on a used Harley FL at a police auction with the intention of doing a 'chop job', he has bought into his share of the hassles, grief and broken knuckles and the frustration of hours of hard work and inevitable mistakes.' In his book entitled *The Rebels: A Brotherhood of Outlaw Bikers*, he went on: 'The practical side of chopping is that it allows a biker to turn a used and inexpensive rat bike (poor condition) into a symbol of power and status.' During the mid-Eighties, the style for rideable street choppers continued to involve rigid and swing arm frames and both springer and telescopic front ends although increasingly newer components were used. Cast alloy wheels, supplied by Harley as original equipment, appeared in greater numbers, as did disc brakes simply because a lot of the secondhand Harleys that were chopped had these items as stock. The aftermarket parts industry adapted its products to suit the evolving motorcycles too: fatbob fenders for FXR frames, strutless rear fenders, and low sissy bars for strutless fenders.

The long, low bikes that had become popular in the San Francisco Bay Area in the early Seventies were still being constructed, although by the mid-Eighties the style had reached its peak. The style had been developed by Arlen Ness, Ron Simms and others in California and became popular all over the USA. By the mid-Eighties bikers were looking for more rideable styles. Bill Gardner of GMA from Omaha, Nebraska, was quoted as saying, about just such a bike he'd recently built, that : "I hate to say it, but

I think it's really kind of dead now. More people are into rideability these days. They want a bike they can get on and ride anywhere. These are really just bar-to-bar bikes. You can't ride them seriously." Arlen Ness built one of the most radical of these style machines in 1985 which was based around an FX Super Glide engine and transmission, although these were modified extensively and the engine was equipped with a

Magnuson Supercharger. The frame and most of the other components were custom-fabricated especially for the project. The style of Low Riders by this time had diversified so far from choppers that, while these machines were undoubtedly custom bikes, they were in fact no longer choppers from the 'high-bars-and-rigid-frames' school of thought. Ness went onto take the style to new extremes when he built an even more

radical scooter with similar lines in its design. The bike was based around a 128 cubic inch V-twin engine. The Bay Area styling in a less extreme form was popular and Harley's FXLR of 1986 was testament to this; its LR suffix designated the bike a Low Rider and it featured a rubber-mounted Evolution engine as well as a 21 inch laced front wheel and a 16 inch solid rear.

The marketing of the Evolution Harleys,

Left: *Keith Chadburn from Cumming, Georgia, astride his rigid Shovel chop. It uses a Paughco frame and a twin disc FLH type front end. The paintwork was by Jerry Ingram.*
Above: *So tall are the apehangers, it is easier to use the rear view mirror when it is underneath.*

the founding of the Harley Owners Group (HOG) – seen by some as an attempt by Harley–Davidson to reclaim the family motorcycling tradition – as well as the increasing numbers of a new generation of 'celebrities' seen on Harleys, seemed to make

Harley–Davidson ownership more than simply desirable; all of a sudden it was the hottest fashion accessory anyone could have. Meanwhile the guys who had stuck with Harley through the bad times were somewhat bemused by the whole turnaround in fashion. They'd been ostracized and shunned for so long by mainstream society, discriminated against and snubbed, that seeing their reason for living turned into a fashion symbol wasn't what a lot of guys wanted. They did *not* dig the pre-ripped jeans and designer T-shirts and were surprised by the smart

Left: *Lou Falcigno of the C&L Hog Shop in Fort Pierce, Florida, built this rigid 93 cubic inch Shovelhead chop in the late Eighties. It uses a 1957 straightleg Harley rigid frame, springer forks, flat rear fender, Sportster tank and has the timeless chopper stance.*

nightspots suddenly welcoming 'bikers'. They had been raised on choppers, flatheads, Knuckles and Pans. We're talking way before even the Shovelheads for many – though they undoubtedly make great chops too – so they didn't need some damn yuppie telling them what was cool. Not for nothing did a new rash of stickers appear: 'If motorcycling was a family thing Harleys would have four doors' as well as the considerably more blunt: 'Die Yuppie Scum'. It was a similar story for the Vietnam Veterans. Sick of being treated badly for their involvement in the war they formed a club with one obvious requirement for membership and flew a patch that left no one in any doubt about who they were or where they had been. Pressure brought to bear by them and others with events such as the run to The Wall – the Vietnam War Memorial in Washington – helped bring the POW/MIA issues to the fore. As the Eighties drew to a close the choppers were still running on the streets and even if some of the prominent builders and shops were concentrating on building Low Riders and modifying Evos, the guys at home were still starting with a rigid frame up on a beer crate, a pile of parts, and the determination to see it through. Daniel Wolf noted that: 'Many of the decisions a biker makes while chopping his hog will reflect a solidifying of his outlaw-biker attitude, especially if his choices fly in the face of what the motorcycle industry would consider standard safety features and technological advancements, and what outsiders consider common sense features. For example, he will have to choose between having a springer front end that uses an antiquated system of cushioning the ride with external springs, and a 'glide' front end with hydraulic shock absorbers that has been used in modern production motorcycles [in the USA, earlier elsewhere] since 1949. If the biker chooses the brute strength and 'boss looks' of the sculptured steel springer over the comfortable-riding but plain-looking glide front end, he makes a strong statement

Above: *Vietnam Veterans have strong views on Jane Fonda's wartime trip to Hanoi.*
Right: *The modified Sportster tank on Lou Falcigno's chop is mounted on the top tube, 'Frisco-style'. It features contrasting styles of paintwork by Streeter from Connecticut.*

within the outlaw community. Along with the choice of forks goes the choice of frames. A biker who runs with a springer front end will also likely choose the smooth classic lines of a rigid frame – affectionately referred to as a 'hardtail' – that has no rear shock absorbers, as opposed to a juice frame that compromises bone-clean looks for the comfort of rear shocks. Fellow bikers again will appreciate the sacrifice that this choice entails: 'Hardtails are for hard a----.' Some of the decisions will involve taking risks; most chopper fanatics run their scooters without front fenders or signal lights. The paybacks a biker faces for taking these risks will vary from having to eat mud when it rains...to having his bike ticketed.' In a rare moment of understanding in his otherwise rancorous book Yves Lavigne summed it up more concisely: 'A chopper, although it looks sleek and graceful, is a bitch of a machine to handle.' Who cares so long as it's a class act?'

1980s Shovelhead

Denny Lueders has owned this Big Twin for a few years although he's been riding choppers for thirty years. He modified this Harley himself, including the frame alterations, and completed it with parts from Butterfield Motorcycles and chroming done by Browns in Kentucky.

Specification

Owner: Denny and
Priscilla Lueders
City: Gretna, Nebraska

General

Year: 1976
Make & model: HD
Shovelhead
Built: Ongoing
Assembly: Owner
Time: 5 years

Engine

Year: 1976
Model: Shovelhead
Rebuilder: Owner
Displacement: 80cu. in.
Modifications: Rebuilt
to displace 80cu. in.
Siftons 440 cam.
Air cleaner: S&S
Pipes: Arlen Ness

Transmission

Type: Four-speed
Year: 1976
Modifications: Polished
Shifting: Foot

Finish

Paint: Owner
Color: Black cherry
Special paint: None

Frame

Type: Swing arm
Year: 1976
Builder: HD and owner
Rake: Increased from
stock
Stretch: None
Other modifications:
Frame downtubes
lengthened 2 1/2 inches,
cut-out front neck

Accessories

Bars: Pullback T-bars
Risers: Integral with
handlebars

Fenders

Front: Custom
Rear: Owner

Headlight: Bates
Tail light: Knightlight
Speedo: Custom mini
Seat: Custom leather
Front pegs: PM forward
controls
Rear pegs: Custom
Electrics: 12 volts
Gas tank: Mustang
Oil tank: Chromed
stock
Primary cover: HD
chromed
Sissy bar: Custom
Mirrors: None

Forks

Type: Telescopic
Narrow Glide
Extension: 4in over
stock
Builder: HD and owner
Special features:
Custom assembly

Wheels

Front: 1982 HD spoked
Size: 19in
Hub: Integral with
wheel
Brake: Disc
Rear: HD Spoked
Size: 16in
Hub: Integral with
wheel
Brake: Disc

1990s

THE HIGH-TECH ERA

THE DECADE STARTED on a high as the two biggest biker bashes of the year, Daytona and Sturgis, reached their 50th anniversaries in the first years and drew record crowds to Florida and South Dakota respectively. Just when it was almost possible to begin to think everything that could be done with choppers had been, something altogether new would arrive on the scene. At the beginning of the Nineties the Evolution engine was proving popular and being used in the construction of traditional rigid-framed choppers and the so-called master builders of the Hamsters MC and others were still concentrating on long, low machines that combined elements of styling from Bay Area Low Riders and the quarter-

Left: *Arlen Ness built one of the first new old-style choppers in 1991 when he put this rigid Panhead together with apehangers and flames.* **Below:** *More typical of late Eighties' and early Nineties' choppers is Nebraskan Bill Bultz's 1975 FX with modified swing arm frame.*

mile drag strip machines. The transition from the Eighties into the Nineties was, like that of previous decades, a gradual one. A good indicator is that magazine feature bikes – usually the cream of the crop – of the early Nineties still included machines which were finished with engraved parts and goldleaf scrolled paintwork, springers and rigid frames are still to be seen.

On the world stage; the various allies who formed the coalition deployed their armies into Saudi Arabia in Desert Shield and later

Above: *Ian Borrowman's Swedish-style Evo chop. This extreme bike features long, widely-spaced fork legs, a rigid frame and a wide back tire on a rim with 120 spokes.*
Left: *Pullback bars bolt through the top fork yoke and the tank is mounted on the top tube.*

Desert Storm to liberate Kuwait from the Iraqi army occupying it. The US Army and Air Force were amongst the coalition forces but unlike Vietnam went in-country with public opinion solidly behind them. They would also later come back to the 'world' to a more welcoming reception. Elsewhere the computer technology that was being combined with lathes and milling machines was

Right: *A Nineties' trend for choppers, especially in Europe, is to combine the Harley V-twin engine and frame with high performance components such as those from sports bikes. This Welsh Outlaw's chopper is at once both traditional and modern.*

Above: *Chris Brown's rigid Shovel features the springer front end and disc brake from one of Harley's springer softail models.*
Right: *The intricate paintwork reflects the rebelliousness of the basic chopper in slogans, flames and skulls.*

the catalyst for change within custom bike building because it enabled the widespread use of billet aluminum for the manufacture of a new range of custom components. All of a sudden there were replacement billet parts for almost every part of a motorcycle. Brake and clutch master cylinders, brake calipers, engine and transmission dress-up items, fender struts, wheels, twistgrips and more. One of the first major exponents of billet parts was Arlen Ness who was also one of the builders that brought old-style choppers back to the forefront of custom biking. He built a rigid-framed Panhead chop which was old-style in shape and silhouette but up

Above left: *This California bike has a modern sculptured shape but is a basic motorcycle in the style of old-time choppers.*
Below left: *Florida's Lou Falcigno built this old-style chop with contemporary components including billet alloy parts and softail frame.*

Above: *This cut-down FXR Evolution is ridden by a probate member of the Sons of Silence MC. It is typical of the Harleys ridden by Nineties' 'One-Percenters' and, while not as showy as some, is certainly true to the old maxim about removing surplus parts.*

to the moment in details including components such as disc brakes and a number of billet alloy parts such as forward controls and master cylinders.

Alongside the steadily increasing use of billet on the Low Rider style of custom bike, the rigid-framed chop was also slowly refined. While Evolution engines and alloy wheels had become commonplace there were still plenty of choppers appearing with Sportster tanks. Increasing numbers of fat-bobs were appearing – rigid and swing arm framed Harley chops with the large capacity old style Harley gas tank. This coincided with the massive boom in popularity of Harley–Davidson motorcycles worldwide. The factory increased its production considerably and exported more motorcycles to more countries than previously. This massive boom in demand had several effects. It increased the demand for accessories and custom parts and so enabled the aftermarket industry based on custom Harley parts to flourish and to expand quite considerably. Manufacturers offering billet alloy parts

multiplied as did those offering components such as custom fenders and handlebars. There were two types of parts manufactured in this boom: bolt-on parts; and the components to construct complete bikes in the chopper tradition if not the style. The bolt-ons were designed for the owners of stock new Harleys who sought to modify their motorcycle without completely reconstructing it. An example is in the 1992 Custom Chrome catalog: Part No. 13-204 Fat Bob Rear Fender Kit for FXR models. This was 'A complete Fat Bob Rear Fender Kit for all FXR models from 1982 through 1986 and 1987 through 1991 FXRTs. The rebellious upswept kick of the chopper-style rear fender is combined with our smooth, chromed steel fender struts that not only improve styling but provide improved fender support over the original equipment parts. Accepts all of CCI's tail light kits with Fat Bob mounts, or the stock (OEM 59993-80) tail light bracket. This kit and its components are not compatible with Original Equipment or aftermarket sissy bars.' This

Right: *Dan Bushey's nostalgia chopper from Acton, California. Although the bike looks like an old-style chopper, it is all-new, based around an Evo engine with Xzotic Pan covers, a Paughco rigid frame and a set of springer forks.*

description leaves no doubt as to which stock Harleys the kit was intended for. Another set of parts were available to do the same jobs to other models such as 13-206 for FXST, FXSTC and FXSTS models from 1984 through 1991. In some ways bolt-on parts such as these kits are the antithesis of the chopper mentality simply because the chopper builder will cut and shut something to fit. As a result 'Custom Chrome Part No. 13-178, a Custom Fat Bob Rear Fender' would be more suited to their bikes as it

Left: *François Bruere's sculptured chopper is based around a Shovelhead engine.*
Below and right: *Although the chopper uses springer forks and a rigid frame, its avantgarde overall appearance is ensured by both the unusual and highly polished gas tank and rear fender.*

came without holes or tail light bracket, leaving the purchaser to drill it to suit his bike. The fact that a fatbob rear fender is included in a large parts catalog at all is of interest and illustrates how established certain fashions are within the world of chopped Harleys.

The fatbob fender came about when early builders used a front fender on the rear of their bikes in place of the original hinged rear fender. The stock front fender on a Harley with springer forks featured and turned out rear lip which when fitted over the rear wheel with the rear edge approximately a quarter rotation up from its original position had the effect of turning up the rear lip of the now rear fender. In the old days this was a straightforward operation because chances are the bike that was about to become a bobber had one fitted when it

was purchased. As the decades pass springer fenders become more scarce so the aftermarket industry had bobbed rear fenders pressed with a cutaway for the drive chain already in place and the advantage of no holes whatsoever, unlike a cut-down stock fender.   Like other parts manufacturers mentioned in this book, Custom Chrome Inc. was established in the early decades of chopper building and as well as the new range of bolt-on parts described above offer components that appeal to chopper builders such as a rigid frame – Part No. 08-914 – for big twins with a neck rake increased by 3° to 33° and two inches extra in the front frame downtubes to accommodate this alteration.

Below: *Pat Kennedy runs a chopper shop in Tombstone, Arizona, where he builds modern choppers, although among their major components are long forks and rigid frames. The gray chopper is Kennedy's own ride while the deep red one is his wife's, Brook's.*

This was one of several variations on nine different frames listed in 1992. That catalog also listed the service parts fundamental to keeping a Harley, stock or chopped, on the road including gasket sets, brake pads and tires. In the same year Minnesota-based Drag Specialties produced a similarly large annual catalog but concentrated more on service parts and accessories. They didn't, for example, list complete frames.

Those who were advertising as manufacturing and distributing custom parts in the early Nineties shows a marked increase over the earlier decades and includes: Sumax, Drag Specialties, Forking by Frank, Antique Cycle Supply, Nempco Inc., Andrews Products Inc., HOG Hollow, Hippy's M/C Parts, KüryAkyn, LBV Engineering, David Sarafan Inc., J&P Cycles, Performance Machine Inc., Mike Corbin, Arlen Ness, Cycle Supply, Superior Motorcycle Parts and Accessories, Tripoli MFG, White Bros, Mustang, Barnett, Cycle Shack, Chrome

Right: *Pat Kennedy set out to create a chopper with an alien theme throughout and fabricated the prismatic components in steel.*
Below right: *The alien theme runs right through to the paint and finish including the creatures and skulls in the detailing.*

Specialties, Delkron, James Gaskets, Jay Brake, Manley, Morris, Paughco, Primo, Rivera, Rowe, S&S, STD, Lightning Cycle Parts, Dragon Precision Machining, Nostalgia Cycle, Graves Plating, Custom Chrome Inc., Samson and Mid-USA Cycle Parts Inc.

The scale of the growing aftermarket parts industry and its phenomenal growth in the early Nineties meant that eventually it was possible to build a complete motorcycle that looked like a Harley–Davidson but used no genuine parts whatsoever. Later companies supplying complete 'American' motorcycles would appear with names including Mirage, Illusion, Big Dog, Titan and more.

Above: *Phil Piper built Shovel Trouble II from scratch around a big twin engine. The chop uses numerous one-off custom parts, including the rigid frame and fat, solid rear wheel.*
Left: *Steve Green's minimalist rigid chop is based on a custom frame and Sportster tank.*

Many of these followed the contemporary style established by the factory big twins but offered more potent engine packages and custom paintwork. The factory was also pursuing nostalgia hard. The springer fork front end had been reintroduced in 1988 for the company's 85th anniversary and, in conjunction with the softail frame that looked like an old time rigid but with the advantage of rear suspension, Harley's new bikes closely resembled those of earlier decades. By the Nineties nostalgia had become a huge market and their bikes looked like Hydra-Glides, Springer Pans, while the Wideglides and Superglides looked like older choppers

Above: *Bjorn, a member of HAMC Kent, England, built this Evo chop around an old rigid Harley frame and Swedish Tolle forks.*
Right: *Jock, a member of HAMC Windsor, England, rides this long-forked chop based around a softail frame and cast alloy wheels.*

and words like Heritage and Nostalgia appeared as model names. The Fat Boy caused a scene, looking like no other factory-built motorcycle and with a name that was an amalgam of the names of two bombs dropped on Japan – Fat Man and Little Boy. Like the T-shirt says: 'Two bombs weren't enough'. This was followed by the FXSTSB Bad Boy, possibly the nearest motorcycle to a Hollister-era bobber any factory could make in the last decade of the 20th century ,hamstrung by laws about turn signals, noise regulations, emission regulations and light laws. Such machines didn't meet with universal approval or acceptance. Snow and

Sager writing in *Iron Horse* magazine in December 1994 felt that 'Milwaukee continues to market its approximation of the outlaw aesthetic to consumers as "genuine" when it's no more authentic than a cereal box reproduction of the Great Masters' works. Only the individual can transform his bike into a real custom.' They went on to say of the Nineties: 'The success of the factory's stunted redefinition of customization can be seen everywhere from so-called custom bike shows to the highways to the majority of Harley mags on the stands.' *Iron Horse* magazine has had quite a mixed history but during the Nineties has stayed both unswervingly true to and also honest about choppers and about the bikers who build and ride them.

With the factory putting springers on their production Harleys it was almost inevitable that springer-forked choppers would see an upsurge in popularity. This was made even more likely with the fashion for a new style of custom Harley – the Luxury Liner. Basically these bikes were 'out-garbaging' the

Below: *A Nineties' version of the all-time classic chopper. It combines a triangular rigid frame, long forks, high bars, Sportster tank, fatbob rear fender, upswept exhaust pipes and flamed paint into the shape of the classic chop. The front disc brake and the Evolution engine look completely in keeping and reflect how newer parts are absorbed by builders.*

Above: *Phil Piper riding the hardtail chop he calls Flame Job. It uses a one-off custom frame into which is fitted a 96 cubic inch S&S V-twin engine. Telescopic forks, alloy wheels and King Sportster tank are also used.*

garbage wagons featuring more bodywork than a stock factory dresser and being as far from a bare bones chopper as it was possible to get without putting four wheels on. The trend sparked an equal and opposite reaction which has seen the dramatic increase in popularity of long-forked choppers again. One major exponent of the revived style with a new twist is Pat Kennedy who runs a shop in Tombstone, Arizona. He had seen the peculiarly Swedish style of choppers built in that country with enormously long telescopic front ends, and he built choppers in that style in the USA.

Suddenly it seemed that in the Nineties anything goes. Low Riders, high performance Harleys, Dressers, Luxury Liners, Garbage Wagons, choppers, nostalgia choppers and billet-adorned stockers were all to be seen. The one thing they had in common apart from V-twin power plants was use of high-tech components and techniques – Mig and Tig welding advanced building techniques for example. The truth is though that fashions go in circles and this is as true in chopper building as in anything else; in the late Nineties the custom market is drifting back into a change for change's sake situation. Oftentimes this is leading to the construction of ostentatious bikes as well as bikes that bear no resemblance to the basic brutal chopper. Part of this is because of the influx of people who want a Harley as a

fashion accessory rather than because they're scooter trash. The latter frequently wears a T-shirt that reads: 'It's not about riding motorcycles anymore. It's a f---ing fashion show.'

The media and law enforcement agencies remain fascinated by the 'One-Percenters' and the major clubs like the Bandidos, Breed, Hells Angels, Outlaws, Pagans and Sons of Silence face continual scrutiny. Despite there being almost half a century of chopper history, as recently as 1994 the best definition of a chopper that the Royal Canadian Mounted Police could come up with in an investigation into outlaw motorcycle clubs was the following: 'Chopper – chopped or cut-down motorcycle. All unnecessary equipment is stripped off the bike including the front brake and fenders. The wheel fork is extended and the handlebars are set high.' There is an irony in this because the type of chopper ridden by the 'One-Percenter' of the Nineties has evolved from the basic chopper of yore. Nowadays it tends to be closer to stock but modified to a distinct style. This reflects both the need for mobility and the distances to be covered. A

Left: *Another style of chopper that became popular in the Nineties was the Taildragger, named for its long rear fender. Some regard these bikes as too ornate to be choppers because of parts like the fender which in the old days was cut back rather than extended.*

Above: *Milwaukee Iron is a chop shop in Lynchburg, Virginia, which has built a variety of unusual choppers in recent years. This nostalgia chop was unveiled at Daytona in 1997. It is an early-style bike with modern touches including discs and billet parts.*

significant number of club bikes can be identified at a glance.

By 1995 Chrome Specialties Inc. from Texas, itself only launched in 1984 by the Kuelbs brothers, had acquired Jammer Cycle Products and included the brand in their 760 page catalog. They weren't alone: Minnesota's Drag Specialties catalog for 1995 numbered 735 pages; New York based Nempco had a 882 page catalog out; while the Custom Chrome Inc. edition for the same year had 768 pages. Part No. 08-914 – the big twin rigid frame – was still listed, proving that despite all the other trends

within the Harley riding spectrum, the chopper builder still thrived. Even now not everyone buys a custom frame. It's still not uncommon to see chops based on modified factory frames be they swinging arm or rigids. While the styles of real choppers vary in detail the overall one remains one based around a rigid or a swing arm frame with a long front end and either a fatbob or Sportster tank. Types and diameters of wheels, lengths and rakes of front ends, and types of rear fenders all vary, as do the type of hubs, brakes, gear shifts, amount of chrome and choice of paint. The latter two finishes vary according to the amount of money the builder wishes (or has) to spend, what his bike is about – 'Chrome don't get ya home' – and what his aims are. There are exceptions. For example, softail frames are used in choppers although some builders really don't like them because they are imi-

tation hardtails, i.e. they are just not real.

The biggest future threat to choppers and their riders is not of their numbers diminishing or the creativity drying up but a more bureaucratic one. The threat is more of being legislated off the road. Already in some European countries it is illegal to modify a motorcycle. In others the laws about modifications are positively draconian and the laws about youngsters riding motorcycles and getting a license are designed to deter rather than encourage. Helmet laws can be seen as the thin end of the wedge. Helmet Laws Suck. Choppers Rule.

1996 Flame Job

This chopper is a contemporary incarnation of the traditional long-forked, rigid-framed chopper, featuring as it does both these major components but use of modern materials, techniques and components such as alloy wheels, disc brakes and billet alloy parts, bring it bang up to date.

Specification

Owner: Phil Piper
City: Leicester, England

General

Year: 1996
Make and model: S & S, 96cu. in.
Built: 1996
Assembly: Owner
Time: Several months

Engine

Year: 1996
Model: S & S
Rebuilder: Owner
Displacement: 96cu. in.
Modifications: Built from S & S long block
Air cleaner: S & S
Pipes: Custom-made

Transmission

Make: Revtech
Years: 1996
Modifications: None
Shifting: Foot

Finish

Paint: Nobby, Leicester, England
Color: Many!
Special paint: Murals and flames

Frame

Type: Rigid
Year: 1996
Builder: Streetfighters UK
Rake: Enough
Stretch: Enough
Other modifications: Made-to-measure frame; trick chain tensioner

Accessories

Bars: Drag extra wide one-off
Risers: CCI

Fenders

Rear: Flat custom
Front: None

Headlight: Bates
Tail light: Cat's eye
Speedo: Mini custom
Seat: Solo
Front pegs: Forward
Rear pegs: None
Electrics: 12volts/CCI alternator
Gas tank: King Sportster with aircraft filler
Oil tank: Santee
Primary cover: None
Sissy bar: None
Mirrors: Custom oval

Forks

Type: Kawasaki telescopic
Extension: 10in over
Builder: Cycle Haven

Wheels

Front: Kawasaki cast alloy
Size: 17in
Hub: Integral with wheel
Brake: Twin Kawasaki discs and calipers
Rear: Custom solid
Size: 16in
Hub: Custom:
Brake: Inboard disc & PM four pot caliper

KNEES IN THE BREEZE

CHOPPERS – a blend of form and function – are about motion, travel, and going from place to place whether it's cross-country or bar to bar. In this they are following the tradition of movement within American society. More than one writer and sociologist has suggested that a proportion of bikers and 'One-Percenters' are bred from the stock of the Okies who migrated west to California to escape the poverty and drudgery of dustbowl life, like the characters in Woody Guthrie songs and John Steinbeck novels. Indeed, H.R. Kaye's biographical book, *A Place in Hell*, recounts that the parents of the book's major character Bill Henderson arrived in Oakland, California, for exactly those reasons. That particular migration was simply one of a series of such migrations. Settlers in North America had been moving west almost since the continent was discovered and later there were the Gold Rush migrations and the long cattle drives. There's the guys who rode coast to coast aboard the box cars, the guys who drive eighteen-wheelers cross-country, and there are the bikers to whom mobility is part and parcel of their existence. Their lifestyle fits comfortably within the American traditions of movement. Even within motor-

Left: *An Eighties' Sportster chopper on the road in the Daytona sunshine. It features girder forks and a twin disc cast front wheel.*
Below: *Bjorn flying his colors on an English highway aboard his Big Twin Evolution-powered rigid chopper.*

Above: *Prof in the classic chopper pose behind the apehangers on his traditional chopper. It features a flathead 45 engine and a four-speed British gearbox fitted into a rigid frame with telescopic forks. Laced wheels and a Sportster tank are also used.*

cycling's short history, the idea of roaming far and wide was established early on. In its earliest days the race was continually on to break trans-continental records and by the outbreak of World War II the concept of the AMA-sanctioned Gypsy Tour was firmly established. Nowadays the biker's vernacular is full of terms and phrases that obliquely refer to that sense of mobility – sled bumming, saddle tramp, cycle Gypsy, scooter trash, iron horse, nomad clubs, being in the wind and more. Some of this colorful terminology is clearly borrowed from the old West and the blues but the meanings are clear enough. It's all about the tires humming on the asphalt.

And hum they most certainly do, espe-

Left: *Steve Green riding his S&S-powered chop. The clean lines afforded by the triangular rigid frame and the way the Sportster tank flows along the top tube are plainly evident here as is the Wide Glide arrangement of the forks with the twin disc laced front wheel.*

cially twice a year for the biggest biker gatherings on the planet. There's Daytona in the early spring to shake off the winter, which still has the northern states firmly in its grip, and soak up some Florida sunshine. Then there's Sturgis in late summer before the fall heralds the arrival of winter in lands special to native Americans, and there's also nearby Deadwood which is famous as one of the haunts of the old-time outlaws. The week's migrations are the annual rendezvous of the biker nation. Some make one or both every year, some only make it out to these places once or twice ever, but it's a special thing to be in town during the bike weeks. Drinking and partying and riding and racing and renewing friendships across the miles. Both

of the events have developed and changed as the decades have passed. There's no racing on the beach in Daytona anymore; the main street in Deadwood isn't knee-deep in beer cans these days; and the partying in Sturgis City Park isn't the spectacle it once was since camping was banned there. Like the T-shirt says: 'To hell with the races, I came to party'. New bars have opened to cater for the growing number of attendees; bikers are perhaps more welcome than they once were and respected more for the money they spend; some of them yuppie women look real fine; and the police are on the whole more tolerant than in the past. With the certainty that day follows night, come March there'll be Harleys and choppers running up

Right: *Sharon and Mark Finstad in Sturgis on his 1942 Knucklehead chopper which features Paughco springers. Mark described himself as "kinda partial to old Harleys."*
Below: *James Brusca on his old-time Knucklehead at Daytona Beach in March 1997.*

Right: *Andy Peters cornering on his chopped-down 1980 FLH Shovelhead. The big, mostly black bike retains its stock forks and swing arm frame but has been lowered and features an array of custom made parts including the forward control footpegs.*

motorcycle events at Loudon in New Hampshire. Then: 'Daytona '81 – Will there be an '82?' asked the cover of the June 1981 issue of *Street Choppers* magazine after a week of zealous policing. "I paid my dues, Daytona Cop Week' read the T-shirts of the embittered. Daytona Beach's anti-topless dancing legislation went into effect one mid-

and down Florida's Atlantic coast and come August they'll be following the twists and turns of the Black Hills roads. There are other runs too: Laconia in New Hampshire; Red River in New Mexico; The Four Corners Run (to where four States' boundaries meet); The Laughlin Run in Nevada; and others. With the exception of Laconia, the others aren't as big or as long established but way back who'd ever have imagined that the annual happenings in Daytona and Sturgis would see more than a half-century? There have been attempts to shut these big events down. For example, a piece of legisla-

Above: *Denny and Priscilla Lueders in Sturgis on Denny's chopped Shovel. The altered lines of the frame are clearly evident.*
Below: *Martin Henderson on his Fifties' fatbob. The clean lines of the stock rigid frame show where custom rigid frames look for inspiration.*

tion that in 1981 placed the Laconia Classic in jeopardy was House Bill 635 introduced by Representative Marshall French of Belknap, New Hampshire. The Bill was publicly acknowledged as an attempt to discourage promoters from scheduling any future

night in December 1981 after a circuit judge refused to postpone its implementation.

Time magazine gave an indication of the prevailing attitudes in 1971 when it asked: 'Has any means of transportation ever suffered a worse drubbing than the motorcycle? In the seventeen years since Stanley Kramer put Marlon Brando astride a Triumph in

The Wild One (1953), big bikes and those who ride them have been made into apocalyptic images of aggression and revolt – Greasy Rider on an iron horse with 74 cubic inch lungs and apehanger bars, booming down the freeway to rape John Doe's daughter behind the white clapboard bank; swastikas, burnt rubber, crab lice and filthy

Below: *The timeless image of an Angel on the highway astride a chopper. In this case it is Jock from HAMC Windsor, England, on his Evolution-powered softail chop. The Hells Angels were prominent amongst the first riders of choppers and it was their influence that led to the chopper being recognized worldwide as a bona fide type of motorcycle.*

denim...As an object to provide linked reactions of desire and outrage, the motorcycle has few equals – provided it is big enough...Anti-social? Indeed Yes.'

A decade later P.J. O'Rourke, writing in *Car and Driver* magazine, summed up the appeal of it all in his inimitable style: 'There is,' he wrote, 'a way that women, women of all ages, look at you when you ride a big H–D. It combines disgust and fascination – as though you were walking around in public with your principal organ of reproduc-

Left: *Simon Bisley on his springer chop to the left of Martin Henderson on his bobber.*
Below: *Tig Leake from Leesburg, Florida, on his classic Seventies' chopper. Based around a rigid frame into which has been fitted a Shovelhead engine and transmission, it retains a stock-style fatbob tank but uses a custom rear fender and forks.*

tion hanging out of your pants, but also as though that organ were an exceedingly large one.' You know how it is: 'When we do right no one remembers – when we do wrong no one forgets,' as the old biker motto says.

Black biker T-shirts frequently feature slogans that are effectively the billboards of the prevailing collective thoughts of the times – political in some cases, lewd and lascivious in others, and frequently cynical, but all designed to raise a smile. A selection from the early Eighties includes the following:

Right: *A classically-styled rideable chopper on the road at The Red River Run in New Mexico. The bike is a modified big twin with custom front fender, seat and sissy bar.*
Below: *A Sportster chop in Daytona, Florida. It features long, raked, twisted leg springer forks. The alterations to the frame headstock to accomodate the forks can be seen.*

Above: *Texan, Dark Star on his traditionally-styled Evo chop at Sturgis in South Dakota. The chopper, built from scratch, uses one of the last Denver's Choppers rigid frames. Dark Star, a custom painter, painted both the base color and the flames on his bike.*

'My Ol' Lady Yes, My Dog Maybe, My Harley–Davidson NEVER', 'Screw imports, buy American', 'Ride Hard Die Free', 'The Surgeon General has determined that messing with a Harley rider is dangerous to your health', 'Rather a sister in a whorehouse than a brother on a Honda', 'Two bombs weren't enough', 'Free Sonny Barger',

'Harleys don't leak oil. They mark their spot', 'Harley riders have longer rods', 'Don't waste gas, waste Khomeini', 'Harley Riders' Ol' Ladies do everything better and look better doin' it', 'Ride a bike. Go to prison', 'It's hard to soar with Eagles when you ride with Turkeys', 'Chrome don't get you home'.

Right: *Just how extreme Swedish-style choppers are is evident in this photograph of Ian Borrowman on his Evolution-powered chop.* **Below:** *Terry Sweeney and Julie on his Knucklehead chopper based on a custom frame and a raked telescopic front end.*

A decade or so later things had changed, but only slightly: 'Pardon me, but I'm a Harley rider and you've obviously mistaken me for someone who gives a s---', 'Ride American, speak English and be proud', 'The older I get the better I was', 'I'd rather have herpes than a Honda', 'Remember when sex was safe and motorcycles were dangerous?', 'You never truly know a woman 'til you meet her in court', 'I'm not easy but we can discuss it', 'If I can't ride my Harley in Heaven I'll ride it straight to Hell',

Left: *Many choppers, including this one at The Red River Run in New Mexico, use custom springer ends. Numerous manufacturers offered custom springers, all of which were basically variations on the original pre-war Harley–Davidson forks.*

'Bikers against Saddam Hussein', 'Sturgis South Dakota – Home of Police Harassment 1993', 'If it ain't rigid it ain't worth a f---', 'You ain't having fun until they dial 911', 'Life ain't easy when you're fat and greasy', 'Live to Ride, Ride to Live', 'Work to Ride, Ride to Work', 'Take a Pride in what you Ride', 'Put your A-- on some Class'.

One thing is for certain, it's been a wild roller-coaster of a ride down the years and looks like continuing to be so. The road goes ever on. Choppers forever.

Right: *Riders leaving the Iron Horse Saloon during Bike Week in Daytona, Florida.*
Below: *Taz, Logie and Charlie on the road in Scotland on their rigid Harley choppers. The popularity of the Harley chopper is now worldwide.*

BIBLIOGRAPHY

Cycle **Magazine**
Cycle Road Test: *Harley–Davidson 1200cc Super Glide*
Ziff–Davis Publishing Company, November 1970

Easyriders **Magazine**
'Wino' Willie Forkner: *All The Old Romance Retold*
Paisano Publications, September 1986

Easyriders **Magazine**
Gary Bang: *A Junkie Hooked On Two Wheels*
Paisano Publications, March 1987

Freedman, J.F.
Against the Wind
The Penguin Group, 1991

Harris, M.
Bikers: Birth of a Modern Day Outlaw
Faber and Faber, 1985

Iron Horse **Magazine**
Look Homeward Angel
J.Q. Adams Productions Inc., December 1994

Jones, J.
WWII
Leo Cooper Ltd., 1975

Kaye, H.R.
A Place in Hell
Holloway House Publishing Co., 1968

Lavigne, Y.
Hell's Angels
Carol Publishing Group, 1987

MacDonald, W.N.
Outlaw Motorcycle Gangs
Royal Canadian Mounted Police Gazette, 1994

Reynolds, F. & McClure, M.
Freewheelin' Frank
Grove Press Inc., 1967

Thompson, H.S.
Hell's Angels
Random House, 1966

Wethern, G. & Colnett V.
A Wayward Angel
Transworld Publishers Ltd., 1979

Wolf, D.R.
The Rebels: A Brotherhood of Outlaw Bikers
University of Toronto Press, 1991

Left: *Styles within the chopper world may come and go but there is little more evocative of what the chopper experience is all about than this image of a long springer forked Harley at night lit only by the light spilling out from nearby bars.*

INDEX

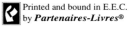
Printed and bound in E.E.C.
by *Partenaires-Livres*®